DISCARD

PUBLICANS AND SINNERS
Private Enterprise in the Service of the Roman Republic

PUBLICANS AND SINNERS

Private Enterprise in the Service of the Roman Republic

E. BADIAN

Cornell University Press
ITHACA, NEW YORK

First published 1972

International Standard Book Number 0-8014-0676-5
Library of Congress Catalog Card Number 70-164712

Printed in New Zealand by
John McIndoe Ltd., Dunedin

Contents

To Rosemary
who came to listen

Preface

When the University of Otago honoured me with its invitation to
deliver the de Carle Lectures in the winter term of its centennial
year, I took the opportunity of discussing a subject in which I
had long been interested, since it is not only of importance to the
student of the late Republic (and particularly to the student of
Roman imperialism and provincial administration during that
period), but one that, even though its importance is generally
recognized, has not had much special attention devoted to it.
Fortunately, and unexpectedly, Ürögdi's article on *publicani* in
the *Real-Encyclopädie* appeared just in time to be of help to me
in the final preparation of the lectures. But my principal debt
(as will be clear on many pages) is to Professor P. A. Brunt's
paper on 'The Equites in the Late Republic', which appeared when
I had just been putting together some thoughts on Roman imperialism, and directed my attention to a field that urgently needed
more detailed enquiry in connection with that subject. That short,
but stimulating and scholarly, paper will be frequently cited in
these pages, with (I think) only occasional disagreement on points
of detail. No one working in this field can further fail to profit
from Professor Claude Nicolet's comprehensive work on the
equites—a mine of learning and information, which we must hope

will soon be made fully accessible by the promised second part and index.

It is a pleasure to thank the University of Otago for its splendid hospitality, which enabled me to work on this subject in a congenial environment and in a peaceful setting rarely found in other countries nowadays; quite apart from seeing old friends again, after many years, and making new ones. It is perhaps invidious to single out names. But the friendly care of the Registrar (Dr J. W. Hayward) and his staff deserves special mention, as does that of Professor J. R. Hamilton (then Acting Head of Classics, now at the University of Auckland); and above all, the interest of my old friend Professor Kenneth Quinn, and the hard work that he put into making the visit both possible and enjoyable, even though in the end he could not stay in Dunedin to hear the actual lectures.

I hope—indeed, I am confident—that the University of Otago, during its second century as during its first, will continue both to play a leading part in the life of New Zealand and to provide an environment in which the arts, the sciences, and scholarship can flourish and find an interested audience.

E. B.

Buffalo, N.Y.
October 1970

Bibliography and Abbreviations

Ancient authors are in general cited according to the Teubner text, except where a different edition is noted (e.g. Clark's for Asconius). Most modern works are cited in sufficient detail to make repetition here superfluous. But several books and articles, repeatedly referred to, are cited either under the author's name only or under an abbreviated title, at least after the first time. For convenience they are listed here.

Badian, E., *Foreign Clientelae (264-70 B.C.)* (1958) [*For. Cl.*]
    Roman Imperialism in the Late Republic² (1968) [*RILR*]
    Studies in Greek and Roman History (1964) [*Studies*]
Brunt, P. A., 'The Equites in the Late Republic', *Second International Conference on Economic History, 1962* (1965), 117
De Laet, S. J., *Portorium* (1949)
Frank, Tenney, *Economic Survey of Ancient Rome*, vol. i (1933)
Greenidge, A. H. J., and Clay, A. M., *Sources for Roman History, 133-70 B.C.*, Second edition, revised by E. W. Gray (1960) [Greenidge-Clay²]
Gruen, E. S., *Roman Politics and the Criminal Courts, 149-78 B.C.* (1968)
Kniep, F., *Societas Publicanorum*, vol. i (1896: all published)
Meier, Chr., *Res Publica Amissa* (1966)
Mommsen, Th., *Römisches Staatsrecht*, vols i³, ii³, iii (1887) [*Staatsrecht*]

Nicolet, Cl., *L'Ordre équestre à l'époque républicaine*, vol. i (1966)

Rostowzew (= Rostovtzeff), M. I., *Geschichte der Staatspacht* (*Philologus, Suppl.* IX 3 (1902)) [Rostovtzeff]

Shackleton Bailey, D. R., *Cicero's Letters to Atticus*, 7 vols (1965-70)

Toynbee, A. J., *Hannibal's Legacy*, 2 vols (1965) [References to vol. ii]

Ürögdi, G., 'Publicani', *RE, Suppl.* xi (1968), col. 1846

Walbank, F. W., *Historical Commentary on Polybius*, vol. i (1957: Books i-vi); vol. ii (1967: Books vii-xviii)

Journals are abbreviated as in *L'Année philologique*, with slight modifications. Standard collections are abbreviated by initials, in the accepted manner. The following should be noted:

CAH = *Cambridge Ancient History*

CIL = *Corpus Inscriptionum Latinarum*

ESAR = *Economic Survey of Ancient Rome*, 6 vols (1933-40), ed. T. Frank

FIRA = *Fontes Iuris Romani Anteiustiniani*[2] (1941), ed. S. Riccobono

ILLRP = *Inscriptiones Latinae Liberae Rei Publicae*. vol. i[2] (1965), vol. ii (1963), ed. A. Degrassi

MRR = *The Magistrates of the Roman Republic*, vol. i (1951), vol. ii (1952), *Supplement* (1960), ed. T. R. S. Broughton

RE = Pauly-Wissowa, *Real-Encyclopädie der classischen Altertumswissenschaft*

SEHHW = M. I. Rostovtzeff, *Social and Economic History of the Hellenistic World*, 3 vols (1941)

SIG = *Sylloge Inscriptionum Graecarum*[3], 4 vols (1915-24), ed. W. Dittenberger

I have added a recent work in the same class:

RDGE = *Roman Documents from the Greek East* (1969), ed. R. K. Sherk

I

Contracts in Peace and War

If the average educated person has heard of the Roman *publicani*, he will know two things about them, both based on references in the New Testament: that they were tax-collectors, and that they were closely akin to sinners[1]—not fit people for a religious leader to associate with. Jesus' solicitude for them is on a par with his solicitude for lepers or Samaritans: paradoxical love for the out-casts of Establishment society.

The person who has a grounding in ancient history will know that the publicans of the New Testament were not real Roman *publicani* at all, but merely their local employees—regarded not only with the natural dislike that all working and earning men and women rightly feel for the tax-collector, but with the peculiar loathing reserved for those who collaborate with the foreign con-queror and grow rich on the rewards.[2] He will also be aware, however, that the *publicani* in the proper sense of the term, during the Republic—and in particular the tax-collectors of the imperial Republic in the age of Cicero—were the curse and the scourge of the conquered nations, largely (if one is to trust some modern works) responsible for the detestation of the Roman name among the subjects of Rome, and perhaps even for the downfall of the Roman Republic. And not only modern works. The historian

Livy, speaking of the first half of the second century B.C., tells us as a well-known fact that 'where there was a *publicanus*, there was no effective public law and no freedom for the subjects'.[3] In Cicero, a century later, they appear (when he is not flattering them for personal or political purposes) as ruthless exploiters, who nevertheless have to be appeased because of their economic resources and political power.[4]

Nor is this story altogether irrelevant and remote—mere 'ancient history'. Like all important historical enquiries, ours is relevant to perennial human problems, which are at least as urgent, at least as much debated, and apparently at least as insoluble, today as two thousand years ago. The terms of the particular case may sound strange, and the accepted prejudices may have shifted; but the problem as such falls into a class that is perhaps one of the most urgent in advanced modern societies: that of the relations between government and private enterprise in the service of the community. It is the constant danger of lack of historical training —such as has unfortunately become more common, and is becoming almost respectable, in some circles today—that a given situation may come to be regarded as God-given, and our prejudices to be erected into moral criteria, with any alternative inconceivable, or thought of only with a shudder. In our age, especially,[5] movement may be equated with progress towards a moral end only too easily regarded as predetermined, and resistance to change—not to mention a proposal to reverse it—can then be regarded as evil or (by the tolerant) as a naive wish-dream. I must therefore begin by inviting the reader to consider some very shocking ideas.

We are all familiar with the naive dogmatism that, in some countries, regards it as wicked that a grocer's shop should be run by private enterprise. Most of us would smile at this, whatever— within our own environment—our political views. But those same people are likely to be shocked that (say) the telegraph service or the water supply, in another society, should be in private hands. And even those who admit this would draw the line at having taxes privately collected. Yet traces of such a state of affairs existed until quite recently—and, for all I know, still may, some-where on this earth. When an eminent Professor of Law at the University of Jena published (as recently as 1896) one of the standard works on *publicani*, he could report that certain municipal taxes in his city were still being farmed out for collection; and that the city of Jena was convinced that this was more profitable to it than the system of direct collection adopted by some other cities.[6] He seriously discusses the advantages and disadvantages, both to the state and to the citizen, of the two systems, even as applied to national taxation. Today we take for granted a very much larger intervention by government (local and national) in our private affairs than even our fathers and grandfathers would have thought acceptable; and all this seems very remote to us. The measure of the distance can perhaps be demonstrated by looking at the remark of a professional ancient historian, writing only a few years ago, in a book that has been (on the whole, deservedly) well received by reviewers and by the public. The author is distressed at the sad spectacle of public taxes being collected for private profit: it causes him real moral pain. 'Private companies, working for a profit, have not the integrity of public servants.'[7]

The naiveté is both engaging and characteristic. What makes it startling is that this is a respected historian, writing on the chief period of his own researches. One thinks of that wonderfully public-spirited example of integrity, the public servant Gaius Verres, with his equally public-spirited public secretaries; and, of course, of countries where even today—as the ancient historian will know, if he is given to travelling beyond the sheltered environment of Western-type English-speaking communities—the public servant expects his private cut from the private citizen expecting him to do his public duty. And one wonders: what about medicine? What more distressing than that human lives should be treated by one who is doing it for profit, and not by the integrity of a public servant? The sentiment is often heard, and my esteemed colleague no doubt shares it. But then, what about the integrity of those who make bread or shoes for private profit? Surely those responsible social tasks demand the public servant. We hear the voice of the dogmatists at whom we started by smiling. Perhaps, though, we begin to see that the problems of history are never irrelevant, at least to those who see them as more than antiquarian exercises. We are as much concerned with drawing the proper line between the proper function of the state and the proper function of private enterprise as any civilization has been. And the study of their interaction in any civilization, if viewed without a pair of very unhistorical blinkers, is bound to be instructive as well as interesting. Let us now return to the Roman Republic.

There would be few more pointless exercises than to try to whiten the reputation of those proverbial black sheep, the Roman *publicani*. Our study must proceed *sine ira et studio*. What we are concerned with is to see how private citizens—for it is of the essence of the *publicani* that they were not part of the government machinery proper—came to acquire a position of such power over the subjects and even over the government of Rome. And we must try to arrive at a fair view of the limits of that power at various stages, and of the measure of their importance in the historical process that led from the Republic to the Empire. We shall have to bear with much detailed discussion: history is not entertainment. The historian can only promise that the end will be kept in view.

I shall not be much concerned with times preceding the strictly historical. When the ancient Mediterranean city state emerges into the full light of history, it is governed, politically, by a small upper class, with a minimum of personnel and machinery.[8] The duties of government are very simple: to maintain the favour of the gods for the community; to defend it against foreign enemies and (perhaps) to enlarge its territory and power; and to keep the peace inside it. Naturally, individual states differ in the importance which they attach to each of these tasks, and in the extent to which they use state (as distinct from private aristocratic) power and resources in achieving these limited objectives. As some city states develop towards democratic institutions—most fully Athens, in the fifth and fourth centuries B.C.—the state assumes increasing importance and expands its responsibilities; and the private wealth of the great families is increasingly depersonalized and channelled through it, on the whole with their co-operation and consent. In fourth-century Athens, we find a highly developed system of taxation (in addition to other public burdens imposed on the rich), and tax-farming is an integral part of it. For the state, in spite of all the responsibilities it has assumed, still has only (on the whole) annually changing magistrates to run it, and the very spirit of democracy—in the ancient sense—distrusts and excludes the impersonal continuity of power that is inherent in a bureaucratic state machine.

This will not concern us in detail and would not concern us at all, were it not for the fact that the similarities between the developed Athenian tax-farming system (which is the only one we really know in Classical Greece) and that of Rome have suggested to some that Rome must have been influenced by the Greeks. This is quite possible: the influence may have come through Etruria at a very early stage, or through the Greek colonies of southern Italy; but it is at present quite unproved. In detail, there are as great differences as similarities, and it can be held that the general similarity of the technique developed owing to the existence of basically similar problems in basically similar societies. I mention the possibility only because one is in duty bound to; though one can do no more with it. One must use one's evidence as one finds it, and the evidence—especially for the early period—is limited enough if one confines oneself to Rome. To go beyond would, at present, be quite illegitimate.

Let us, then, confine ourselves to Rome, and start with first principles. There were two kinds of service that the Roman state needed to have done and could not perform for itself. One was the provision of supplies—for religious ritual, for the army, for secular civic purposes (e.g. public buildings), all needed so that the state should perform its proper minimal duties. Of course, these supplies had to be paid for, as soon as the state as such was more than the circle of aristocratic families composing its governing class. And so the state needed money to pay for them; and this led to the other kind of service: the collection of that money needed to pay for the essential state services. With state machinery minimal, both sides of the public ledger were at least to some extent in private hands. What must be repeated, in the face of such startling (yet typical) examples of prejudice and dogma as we have noticed, is that this is perfectly simple and neither surprising nor—from any moral standpoint—reprehensible. Just as some modern states regard all (and all modern states some, and indeed an increasing number) of the economic operations of society as their proper sphere, even though practical considerations temper whatever the ideal happens to be, so the early Roman Republic did not regard economic operations as, in principle, in its sphere at all—even though, for reasons that nobody bothered to expound in theoretical form, some were traditionally exercised. On the whole, it was the *publicani* who supplied economic services—as indeed, to some extent, their successors still do in any non-Socialist state and some that consider themselves Socialist. The very appellation of the *publicani* is due to the fact that they dealt with the public property (*publica*) of the Roman People.[9]

Our firm evidence on contracts for public works and services goes back, indirectly, at least to the beginning of the fourth century B.C. As is known, no Roman history was written before about 200 B.C. The details of earlier history were often freely invented by later writers in the light of contemporary interests and conditions.[10] Livy, in describing the arrangements for the building of early temples, uses language that seems to show him as conceiving of its being carried out by contractors, as in later days; and he uses the same language in the case of the only secular building, as well as in the case of other building tasks.[11] Are we entitled to believe it? As we have seen, on *a priori* grounds it seems likely enough. The only conceivable alternative, for early Rome, would be for the work to be done by the private households of the ruling families; and for this—unlike the contracting system—there is no evidence whatsoever. But we have more positive arguments.

One of the first contracts the censors were traditionally bound to let in the late Republic was that for feeding the sacred geese on the Capitol. The geese had distinguished themselves by raising the alarm when the Gauls took Rome around 390 B.C.[12] The contract must go back as far as that, and quite probably further: the geese had been there, sacred to Juno, when they saved the city—and hardly without official rations. Presumably the contract for feeding antedates their service. The contract for the signal summoning the centuriate assembly must obviously be as old as the assembly itself, which traditionally went back to King Servius.[13] Again, in Classical times senators were debarred from public contracts (we do not know since when), but they were permitted to bid for the supply of horses and chariots for the games in the Circus: C. Antonius, Cicero's colleague in 63 B.C., had bought this contract.[14] Now, the first games in Rome seem to go back to the first half of the fourth century B.C.[15] No doubt that was long before the removal of senators from public business contracts; and the sacred nature of the task prevented abolition of their right to it when the law was changed. There is good reason to think that other contracts with sacred associations may have remained open to them.[16] We can be quite sure, then, that public contracts were being let, as a matter of course, by the fourth century B.C., and fairly confident that they probably were a century earlier and perhaps even under the kings. Since this is so, there is no reason to doubt that Livy's reports on the building of early temples can be accepted as essentially correct; and no good reason to deny that what little secular public building there was would be arranged in the same way. The *publicani* were an integral part of the *res publica* as far back as we can observe it or trace it back.

Contracts for army supplies are first mentioned in the war against Hannibal, but in a way that implies that they were a long-standing institution. The mention is due entirely to the fact that at the time (215 B.C.) conditions were exceptional. In a time of unprecedented fiscal stringency, those who had made profits out of supplies for the war were asked to furnish what was needed for the armies in Spain on credit: the contracts included food, clothing, and 'whatever was needed in addition, for the navy'.[17] Payment was to be made as soon as the Treasury had some money. Three companies— nineteen men altogether[18]—were prepared to bid. But they insisted on exceptional conditions in return: freedom from military service for the time of the contracts; and public insurance for all supplies once they were put on board ship. The praetor had to accept the terms. We do not hear whether he also undertook to pay interest until payment of the sum due was made: this is very probable, especially since there was no security whatsoever, and with the high interest rates normal in antiquity (especially in times of crisis), businessmen probably could not afford to wait for years without getting any money at all. However: the whole process shows that the selling of such contracts was the only known way of getting supplies, and that it had been systematized into set forms. The auction was held by the praetor when supplies were needed. (Of course, it could as well have been a consul, except that the consuls were busy fighting.) The bidders are already associated in companies. Whether bidding was normally competitive we cannot tell: that it was not, on that exceptional occasion, proves nothing. We must note, too, that all risks of carriage were normally borne by the supplier and not by the state: the measure agreed to on this occasion is exceptional; and even so, only sea transport was guaranteed by the state. Presumably the risk on land was small, since the companies did not even ask to be relieved of it: along the main roads, beyond Hannibal's reach, Italy was well policed. But at sea, particularly in wartime, the risk was by no means negligible: in fact, with ancient ships as we know they were, the risk would be high at any time. This must be borne in mind when we think of private profits being allowed on such operations. Unfortunately we have no figures for these particular transactions. We shall come to see at least a glimmer of light in view of later evidence. But, as usual, our sources are more interested in moralizing than in economic history. Let us note Livy's enthusiasm over the contractors' patriotism: 'Such was the character and the love for their country which at that time seemed uniformly to pervade all classes.'

When he wrote this, Livy was probably not yet aware of the sequel.[19] Two years later,[20] it was discovered that two of the nineteen gentlemen concerned had defrauded the exchequer by putting worthless goods on board unseaworthy ships and claiming the insurance sum for army supplies when the ships sank—the method seems highly up to date. The Senate, interestingly enough, refused to act against them, when the matter came to its notice, since it realized the State's dependence on the contractors and wanted to avoid offending them at a time of crisis. So, at least, we are told. Two tribunes tried to act through the popular assembly, but the meeting was broken up by a mob led by the contractors. Thereupon the Senate took firm action, which led to the punishment of all the evildoers.

It is noteworthy that the guilty men were very eminent Romans —both from Etruria, where many Roman families had been settled on conquered land and natives enfranchized. One, T. Pomponius of Veii, was a fairly successful *praefectus socium*: he seems to have raised a volunteer army against Hannibal in southern Italy, but in the end was defeated and captured.[21] We cannot tell how much of the hostile presentation in the story as we have it in Livy is due to prejudice caused by his insurance fraud. The other man, M. Postumius of Pyrgi, who (or whose friends) started the riot at the assembly meeting, was actually related to a tribune of the year, who, however, refused to intercede on his behalf.[22] Both men must be *equites,* men of the upper (officer) class of Roman society,[23] whom we shall later see prominent among *publicani.* It is interesting to see them emerge on the first occasion when there is reference to a supply contract in our sources.

The incident, at first sight, looks alarming, confirming the wisdom of critics of the system. It shows the *publicani,* on practically their first explicit appearance in our record, already organized as an extra-legal pressure group, already putting private profit above the public interest, and willing to defend a member of their class, no matter how bad his case. But we must not exaggerate. Other nations have had their illicit profiteers in wartime, have punished them, and have survived. We must not forget that, out of the nineteen men involved in the contract, only two had taken part in the fraud: there is no reason to think that, once the facts came to light, other malefactors remained undiscovered. This is not a bad record. There are few nations where it would be surpassed among (say) senior civil servants. As for the punishment of the guilty, that story needs scrutiny: as we have seen, the actual history was written in the late Republic, often in the light of contemporary events.

First, the Senate's pusillanimous unwillingness to offend the class of *publicani.* This assumes—as indeed the sequel in Livy

does—the existence of an organized *ordo publicanorum* with the
sort of status and powers that it had in the age of Cicero. Yet the
story arouses doubts. We are told—vaguely—that the Senate had
refused to act 'in the previous year'; and that therefore two tribunes
took the case to the People, obviously at the very beginning of the
new consular year, since the incident appears to have impeded the
consular levies for the year. Yet, after the riot, the Senate is far
from pusillanimous. We may discount the impassioned Livian
oratory; but the fact remains that the same tribunes who had
launched the original prosecution are later chosen as the instruments of the Senate's severity in dealing with the consequences. If
we separate fact from interpretation, we arrive at a consistent
picture: the Senate, informed of the alleged fraud by the praetor
(probably near the end of the consular year), refuses to act; at
the very beginning of the next consular year (not the tribunician
year, which began three months earlier!), two tribunes launch a
public prosecution; when the assembly is disrupted, the Senate,
led by one of the new consuls, takes firm repressive action, which
it entrusts to the same two tribunes. The obvious interpretation,
shorn of its late Republican trimmings, is that the Senate refused
to discuss the matter at the end of a year, in the absence of the
consuls. (Note that it was the praetor who raised the matter.) It
was better to wait for the new consuls to be present, on a matter
of such public importance. Fear of offending the *publicani* cannot
easily be assumed when it is so conspicuously absent later. Nor
was the Senate a court of law. If the matter were discussed, all
that it could do was to decide that the alleged criminals should be
prosecuted. And, of course, prosecuted they were, by two tribunes
—the same two tribunes who, later, are supported by the Senate
and become its instruments of punishment. There is no reason
to doubt that the tribunes had throughout acted as the Senate's
instruments, as tribunes normally did. The unwillingness of that
other tribune, the relative of one of the accused, to veto the trial
is also most easily explained if the trial was not merely a private
venture by two colleagues, but taking place on the instructions of
the Senate. The rewriting of earlier history in the light of the
politics of the late Republic can fortunately be almost demonstrated from the facts of the story.

In the circumstances, the riot organized by the 'class' of
publicani also comes under suspicion. Just as the Senate in fact,
when it comes to a major conflict, shows no fear of them, so we
may assume that there was nothing to be afraid of. Again, we

may accept the fact of the disruption of the meeting. But we need not assume that anyone other than the friends and clients of the two accused—both, as we have seen, powerful members of the upper class—organized the trouble. We are explicitly told that *all* those concerned in the riot were tried and (if guilty) punished, apparently with death or exile, and with confiscation of their property which would go with the capital penalty. Yet it is absurd to imagine that the whole 'class' of *publicani* was thus treated— or needed to be. Contracts had to continue, and did. The riot, like the fraud, was clearly a relatively minor incident, which the Senate and People of Rome proved well able to deal with along established lines. It is only later rewriting that has created the alarming picture of private class power and irresponsibility, and official irresolution.

Contracts inevitably continued. Even before this, we have our first detailed mention of another kind of contract.[24] In 214, still under the pressure of financial exhaustion, the censors had to stop selling contracts for keeping the sacred buildings in repair and for supplying horses for use in processions and games and, we are told, for 'similar things'. (We can only guess what these are; but presumably other sacred services, like feeding the geese on the Capitol: this element appears to be what the two contracts mentioned have in common.) Now, it was more than ever essential, in the course of a dangerous war, that sacred services like these— procuring divine favour—should be maintained. Those accustomed to bidding at the auctions for these contracts therefore suggested that they would do what needed to be done on credit and not ask for their pay until the end of the war. Clearly, the sums involved were relatively small; else the offer could not have been made, at a time when no end to the war was in sight and capital must have been in short supply, with Italy devastated by the enemy. One might regard the story as slightly suspect, since it comes in a catalogue of similar acts of public spirit by all classes, such as Livy is fond of and his predecessors no doubt also were. But since it is not brought into contrast with any other event (Roman disaster or, e.g., the ship fraud by the two contractors), we may accept at least the outline of the story: it bears no positive marks of patriotic invention. We may use it to prove, once again, that public contracts were well established and that there were people who made a habit of bidding for them, even though one can safely assume that they were not totally dependent on them for a living. And we may probably also conclude that the system was working well enough, under what must have been almost intolerable strain.

If we do not hear more about contracts, we may take it that this was why: they were working well, and taken for granted. After all, we hear little about even major supply contracts in the histories of *modern* wars (written by scholars more interested in economic history than Livy and his predecessors were), as long as nothing unusual (such as a major fraud) happens. The State, with its simple machinery,[25] could not have carried out the conquest of Italy and most of Sicily, the building of roads, aqueducts, and temples, indeed all the business of an expanding imperial power, without contracts like those we have been examining. They were taken for granted, and a class of people had inevitably grown up, who expected to make part of their living—we shall see that it was not the whole of it—by means of such contracts.[26] All this we can only posit—safely enough, on both probability and evidence—in general terms.

It is only in 209 B.C. that, quite exceptionally and by a lucky chance, we get at least a very rough idea of the sort of sums involved in all this. As so often, our text is bedevilled with diffi-culties; but it is better than the complete blank we have in other cases.

It was in that year that the Senate decided[27] to use for the war a sum of about 4,000 lbs of gold—the proceeds of a tax on the freeing of slaves, which was levied at the rate of 5 per cent on the value of the slave, and which had been allowed to accumulate for some time, for use as a reserve in a time of dire emergency. (We have seen how desperate the financial situation had become even a few years earlier.) Of this money, some went to the consuls, to two proconsuls and to a praetor in the field; the rest was assigned for army supplies to be sent to Spain. Livy's text and language are difficult to disentangle, and the size of 'the rest' can be differ-ently worked out. Some make it 1,400 lbs; a different reading pro-duces 1,150.[28] In any case, the scale (as distinct from the details) of the operations concerned emerges clearly enough. In Spain, Rome at the time had the equivalent of three or four legions.[29] Livy mentions only clothes to be purchased: presumably food could be obtained on the spot. At the time of the emergency in 215, there had been two legions in Spain, and we can now begin to calculate the cost of clothing for a legion (within fairly wide limits of tolerance, I repeat: the uncertainties of our tradition do not permit certainty in our conclusions), and get some idea of the amount of capital involved. We can see that, to allow for the textual variants, the cost of clothing for a legion was in the range of $287\frac{1}{2}$ (1,150 for four) to 467 (1,400 for three) pounds of gold, i.e. (to reckon by the later Roman coinage)[30] about 290,000 to 470,000 denarii: our mean value is about 380,000. Since in a normal year there were four new legions (often more in the Hannibalic War, and many retained under arms), the total value for their clothing would normally come to about $1\frac{1}{2}$ million denarii, or (in the more common way of reckoning) 6 million sesterces (4 to a denarius).

It will be clear that this is only a very rough guess, meant to represent a range of figures that, although permitting a fair amount of variation owing to the uncertainty of our sources, is yet far from totally arbitrary: we may safely assert that it is not, e.g., likely to be twice or half as much as the true value. As it happens, our meagre tradition allows an unexpected cross-check. The elder Cato boasted[31] that, as an officer and commander, he always bought the cheapest food and clothes; the context implies that they were those of the common soldier. And he mentions that the clothes never cost him more than 100 denarii. That was well after the time we are dealing with; but we have no reason to think that there had been a major change. We may take it that 100 denarii will be an approximation to the cost of an ordinary soldier's clothing. For a legion of standard size (4,200 men)[32] we thus get a total of about 420,000 denarii—in view of the uncertainty of the evidence, remarkably close to the mean of our first calculation. While attaching little value to the precise figures, we may have full confidence in the range we have established.

With the cost of clothing for the normal army so high, we begin to understand the full meaning of Livy's statement that profits had been made out of the war, and the interest of Rome's upper class in these contracts. A further calculation—subject to the same cautions—may now be attempted. In 215, there were at least two legions in Spain. The contract for clothing alone (and we must remember that there was also food, plus supplies for the fleet) must have come to at least 800,000 denarii. For the 19 men who shared in it, this means an average share of over 40,000 denarii. We may recall that in the late Republic—we do not know precisely since when—the property qualification for Equestrian status was 100,000 denarii *of capital;* while the qualification for the first census class, which had the main power in the centuriate assembly, appears to have been a mere 10,000.[33] It is quite probable that the extraordinary contracts of 215, for a single army, amounted (if we allow for the food and navy supplies) to a capital commitment equal to the whole of the later qualification for Equestrian status, for each of the partners concerned.

It would be interesting to know whether normal army contracts were let by the censors—i.e., on an average for five years at a time—or by the annual magistrates. Unfortunately we cannot tell. In the Hannibalic War, at any rate, most of them would have to be let on an annual basis, as the number of legions and armies from one year to the next could not easily be foreseen. Even on an annual basis, however, the capital commitment was considerable. Of course, profit is in a way more important than turnover or capital employed; and this we have no way of judging. To some extent it must have depended on competition; for the government (particularly at a time of crisis, when speed was important) could not afford to withdraw the contracts and try to re-let. And in the crisis of 215 there was obviously no competition. Still, we again have a chance of a rough check on profits. We have seen that Cato's price agrees surprisingly well with the size of the contract for clothing that we have independently established. Since Cato's price was a free market price, this seems to indicate that the profits on the contracts were not excessive. For what little this rough check is worth, it confirms our general impression that the system was working well.

We have not yet commented on the *publicani* as tax-farmers: the role in which they are best known. The fact is that, although they obviously must have obtained part of their profits from this part of their activities, the evidence suggests that at this time taxes were much less important than *ultro tributa*. The main tax on citizens was the *tributum*, a small property levy (one tenth per cent), which the State collected without them.[34] It was the aim of the State to repay any extraordinary levy (frequent in a major war) additional to this as money from other sources (tribute, booty, indemnities) became available. But in any case, the *publicani* had nothing to do with it. Aside from this, there was the 5 per cent tax on manumissions, which we have noticed: it had produced the 4,000 lbs of gold in the Treasury. We have no idea how long it had taken to produce that sum. The tax was introduced in 357, and it has been maintained that it took the whole of the intervening 150 years to produce the sum mentioned.[35] But this is demonstrably untrue, since at its institution the tax (we are told) was intended to pay for current expenses, and we have no information on when it was assigned to its special purpose. Nor do we know whether that sacred treasure had been used before (e.g. in one of the dire emergencies of the First Punic War); and if so, whether the money had been replaced after. There is little point in guessing. However, even if we assume that the treasury had been built up entirely since the beginning of the war, in (say) ten years—which is highly unlikely—the annual sum collected comes to only 400 lbs of gold (i.e. 400,000 denarii); and profits on its collection cannot have been very high. Finally, there were no doubt *portoria* (customs and especially harbour dues). These first appear in our sources at the very beginning of the Republic, when we are told that the newly supreme Senate relieved the Plebs of them, in order to ensure its loyalty.[36] The story, like most stories about the early Republic, is almost certainly a late fiction. It is hard to imagine that this fact could have been authentically transmitted over the intervening centuries. However, in any case there is no mention of such dues for centuries after; and if the abolition is historical, it was obviously long-lasting. If any such taxes were collected by 200 B.C., we do not know of them, and they cannot have been important.

Related to taxes were rents paid to the State for public land. Unless wanted for other purposes (e.g. the foundation of a colony, or, as by C. Flaminius, distribution to Roman settlers in individual lots), public land was normally occupied by private persons for varying uses, against payment of a tax.[37] However, at the time we are dealing with (the Hannibalic War) there cannot have been much public land left in this condition: C. Flaminius, in 232 B.C., had probably given away the last major stretch not previously colonized. Rents from this source, therefore, cannot have amounted to much.[38] The only other regular source of profit for the *publicani* that we know of was the sale of salt, which was always a public monopoly. We happen to know that the price of salt was increased during the Hannibalic War, outside the city of Rome only.[39] But since that price had been—and in Rome remained— one *as* (the smallest bronze coin, one tenth of the denarius when the latter was established) for six pounds, it is clear that no fortunes were made out of its sale.

It is therefore fair to say that, at the time when Rome was emerging victorious from the Hannibalic War, the profits from tax-collecting were small. The publican's chief profits came from the *ultro tributa* (contracts for goods and services, especially army supplies); and there it is quite possible that even minimal profits would, as Livy says, make large fortunes, when the number of legions was increased from the normal four to over twenty, while the emergency whittled away competition and put the government at the mercy of the contractors. As we saw, there were (as was to be expected in such conditions) odd cases of dishonesty, at elevated social levels that made the affair alarming. But we have also seen that profits were, on the whole, probably not excessive; and both the little positive information that we have and the silence of our sources—which spread themselves on the scandal of the two dishonest contractors—must be taken as sufficiently showing that the hundreds of contracts that were made all the time, in order to keep the war effort going, must have turned out well enough. On the whole—and it is an impressive whole—the *publicani* of this period did their jobs well. The support shown for the two malefactors is said to show a class solidarity that might be regarded as socially dangerous; but we have seen reason to doubt the accuracy of the details in that whole story, which may well have been dramatized and interpreted in the late Republic. In fact, whoever it was who dared to break up an assembly of the People, they failed in their attempt. The Senate and People, cooperating through the tribunes, were firmly in control. And the incident aroused no real alarm and did nothing to change policy.

II

Expansion and Conflict

The Hannibalic War was immediately followed by the major wars in the eastern Mediterranean, which resulted in the extension of Roman power and influence—though without annexation—over the whole of that area within a decade or so. In the last decade of the third century Rome had been fighting for her life against an enemy who was not easily dislodged from a position on her own doorstep. Only one generation later, Rome's supremacy over the whole Mediterranean area was unchallenged, and the distant successors of Alexander the Great were sending their embassies to Rome, to let the Senate decide their fate by its support and recognition. In this world of suddenly and vastly expanded horizons, the business of state contracting naturally saw a corresponding expansion.

The number of legions was never anywhere near the peak attained during the Hannibalic War. However, with constant fighting in Spain added to the major wars in the East, it was well above what had been normal before that War.[1] Moreover, the fighting now took place at large distances from Rome, so that the sums employed would be correspondingly larger. There was also a tendency, certainly by about 170 B.C., to increase the size of the individual legion. It has been worked out—admittedly as a rough estimate

—that the average number of citizens under arms in each year from 200 to 157 B.C. was 47,000.[2] It is important to stress that, as far as we can see, the *publicani* were in charge of the commissariat for all these wars, providing the logistics and the organization that enabled the legions to win them; just as, in the grimmest days of the war with Hannibal, they had got supplies through to the troops, sometimes—as we saw—without much hope of payment. Their misdeeds are on public record; they ought to get the credit for a series of achievements that tend to be forgotten.

Of course, the problems were not as complicated as in the case of a modern army. The great Alexander, as far as we can see, had managed to win his vast empire with only the most rudimentary organization of supplies and communications, by living off the land wherever he went. But we have already seen that this was never entirely so in the case of the legions. Naturally, some food and equipment would be captured in usable condition. But we saw what large contracts had to be let, in the Hannibalic War, to supply the forces fighting in Spain; we shall see the same true of the wars in the East a little later. Even in the days of Pompey, forces in Spain had to be supplied from Italy. The reason why we do not hear more about all this is simply, as before, that when the system was functioning normally, it was taken for granted: nobody was interested enough to comment on it unless things went wrong. The routine of contracts and supplies was (and still often is) beneath the notice of the gentlemen writing the history of politics and campaigns.

This has to be said at length because the standard English treatment of these matters gives a very different impression. Tenney Frank states[3] as a matter of fact that, as a result of the insurance fraud in the middle of the Hannibalic War, 'in the subsequent wars in the East the state always seems to have bought its supplies through its own magistrates who provided the transport'. He does not give us any idea of how the magistrates suddenly acquired the technique and the organization that enabled them to manage the complicated business of buying supplies and providing transport. Did the State itself now go into the contracting business? If so, who were the magistrates concerned in it; how did they do it in addition to their normal duties; and why did the State opt out of the business again later? Four passages in Livy are alleged in evidence.[4] All of them, on inspection, deal with the same kind of thing: the imposition of a second ten per cent contribution of grain (*alterae decumae*) on the chief grain-producing areas, against payment, and its transport to wherever it was wanted (Rome or a theatre of war). It is easy to find precedent for this at an earlier time, and in the middle of the Hannibalic War.[5] The organization of the grain supply for Rome in Italy was the traditional business of the quaestors. In the provinces concerned, the imposition of the second tithe merely used (as we see in the case of Verres' Sicily) the machinery already established for the tribute tithe. In all these cases, machinery already existed—no doubt of different kinds: there is every reason to think that that in Italy was as different from that in Sicily as that in most other provinces was; and that machinery was used simply because it was there—not out of any new distrust felt towards the *publicani*. Indeed, when we are told that a praetor was to see to the transport of that grain to another area, there is no implication that he was to transport it on warships under his command. Presumably, in most cases, he would not even have a sufficient number of ships. What he would do is not difficult to imagine: just as for the transport of clothing, both in 209—only a few years after the great insurance fraud—and, as we shall see, in the great wars in the East, he would let a contract for having it shipped. In fact, where no special tithe was imposed, we may well believe that even the supply of food might be left to contractors, just as it had been in 215—not to mention its transport. In 195 M. Cato found food-supply contractors firmly established, as of right, in the Spanish theatre of war.[6] It is strange that a standard work could so readily generalize from a few cases of an imposed contribution of grain, collected through existing official machinery, to a total exclusion of *publicani* in the procurement and transport of all military supplies, where no such machinery existed.[7] In fact, Tenney Frank was aware of some of the actual evidence to the contrary. He admits that in what he calls 'the small contract for horses and military garments in 167' [read 169] the *publicani* 'may have been employed (Livy, 44, 16) as intermediaries'. In fact, Livy admits of no doubt: a contract for 6,000 togas, 30,000 tunics and 200 Numidian horses (including their transport to Macedonia) is let by a praetor at Rome, while grain is bought from the Epirots on the spot. Not only is the reference to the contract explicit, but it is actually stipulated that delivery has to be made to any place in Macedonia chosen by the Roman commander. It is difficult to see what—other than unwillingness to admit error—led Tenney Frank to put his admission in such hesitant form. And if on that special occasion, we have to ask: why not normally? Tenney Frank must surely have been aware of that. The only reason why the whole business is mentioned is because it is exceptional in one respect: not the normal letting of supply contracts, but business taken out of season, in response to an urgent appeal from a Roman commander, who had probably suffered unforeseen losses. Had there been public machinery for obtaining and moving such supplies, we cannot doubt that it would have gone into action at once, to cope with the emergency. When we see the machinery of the *publicani* called up to do so, we are forced to conclude that it was they—and not the State—who ran the normal machinery for such things: just as they had run it back in 209, when an even more exceptional occasion had called on them for even more exceptional steps.

Trying to belittle the part of the *publicani* at this time, Tenney Frank incidentally calls the emergency contract 'small'. So, of course, it was, compared with the regular supplies for the (at least) eight legions that we may regard as normal at this period. But let us not be misled by that comparison into absolute assertions. We must try to establish some figures, approximate though they will be.

We have seen that a soldier's clothing might cost 100 denarii.[8] Let us allow half of this for the toga, an elaborate and heavy garment. The rest would be divided between tunic and shoes; let us again, as an estimate, allow half for each. This rough distribution gives 50 denarii per toga and 25 per tunic. If not precise, these estimates must be in the right range. We can now work out that the 6,000 togas would cost 300,000 denarii and the 30,000 tunics 750,000 denarii. (It is interesting to see, by the way, that a supply of five tunics was carried for every toga. We have no reason to think this proportion exceptional.) So the total for the clothing alone comes to over a million denarii. For horses, we have no reliable information: only the official cavalry allowance of 500 denarii, in the third century.[9] Of course, the rare Numidian horses here specified are bound to have cost a good deal more: they may well have had to be actually imported from Numidia. An estimate of 100,000 denarii (i.e. the value of the third-century allowance) is likely to be ridiculously low. However, the total estimate for this 'small' emergency contract comes to 1,150,000 denarii on our computation. When we recall that at this time the soldier's pay was perhaps 120 denarii per year (minus deductions),[10] we see that the contract was equivalent to the annual pay for 10,000 men. Or again, to put it in terms of class qualifications we have already noted, it was equivalent to the *property* (not income) qualification of about a dozen Roman knights! Proper attention to this 'small' contract proves illuminating as to the scale of the contracting business during the great wars of the early part of the second century. What it does not tell us, unfortunately, is the number of people or companies concerned, or the rate of profit as opposed to capital employed. Again, the Latin historian was not interested in such things, which to us would be of greater interest than much of what he gives us. But we shall soon see that a large number of people took part in the contracts; and presumably even a small profit, where the scale of operations was so large, must have added up to large fortunes being made by some people.

The booty of the eastern wars flowed back to Rome; and the quantity—which has often been tabulated—makes an astonishing list: down to 167 B.C. (where we lose Livy's text), Frank has worked out[11] a well-founded estimate of 70 million denarii from the East alone, with perhaps 40 million from other theatres. This fantastic total of 110 million denarii[12] is, of course, only the public booty, surrendered to the Treasury. In addition, sums that cannot even be conjectured went to hundreds of thousands of individual Romans: soldiers, officers, commanders, benefiting in steeply increasing proportion. The law and custom of Rome were generous in allowing individual commanders a great deal of discretion on how to deal with booty taken in war,[13] and we may be sure that the total infusion of money into the Roman economy over this period was many times the amount received by the State. However, it is this last that now chiefly concerns us.

Rome had a long tradition of not, on the whole, using taxpayers' money for public works, but—wherever possible—relying on the spoils of war to pay for them. Hence the influx of booty meant a vast increase in public building. The amounts spent are—as nearly always!—unknown. But we do have the significant fact that the Senate, at least on occasion, now made regular allocations of public revenue for this purpose—no doubt because most of the money was no longer coming from Roman taxpayers. In 179 the censors received a year's public revenue for their building contracts; in 169 half a year's.[14] This is all the information we have on the subject. It shows that the amount available varied. (In 169, we must remember, a major war was going on in Macedonia.) But in view of Livy's known carelessness about such matters, we may take it that at this time—even though it is not mentioned for the census of 174, which in fact was associated with a lavish building programme[15]—a large proportion of the public revenue was regularly devoted to building. Since we do not have Livy's text for any censorship after 169, we cannot tell how long this went on. However unsatisfactory Livy is as a historian, a glance at the pages of the standard work on *The Magistrates of the Roman Republic* will show how helpless we are as soon as we lose his guidance: there are now, for over a generation, only odd snippets in a variety of sources, none of them interested in more than its own tiny fragment of the events concerned. However: when we begin to get more information, in the age of the Gracchi, major censorial building is not mentioned and must have stopped. Still, while it was going on, large sums were obviously spent on it.

There was more building going on than was let by the censors. Thus in 196 the aediles put up some buildings, and this is also recorded on some later occasions—again, we may not assume that Livy's coverage is complete.[16] The aediles regularly used money from fines (*de pecunia multatica*) for such purposes; and though usually it was only enough for a statue or two, it would often stretch at least to a minor building: a shrine, say, or a portico.

Again, Frank (followed by Toynbee) takes this building by the aediles to have by-passed the *publicani* and mentions it as a sign of (apparently intermittent) 'periods of distrust' of them.[17] He fails to ask himself how the aediles in fact did put their buildings up: hardly with their own hands, nor even—as far as we know— through their own slaves. The answer, of course, is that they let contracts for the building, and such contracts are referred to in surviving documents.[18] No such activity, in fact, can be imagined without the intervention of contractors.

There is no point in going through all the other classes of contracts in which we now find the *publicani* engaged: the classes are much the same as before, but the opportunities are greater. One new category is worth mentioning: the state mines. We do not know of any mines owned by the Roman People before the Hannibalic War. During the War, important mines were captured from the Carthaginians in Spain. These were probably exploited as state property by the Carthaginians; for it is generally true that the Romans took over the kind of administration of conquered territory and property that they found. In any case, the Romans made these mines public property. There can be little doubt as to how the mines were to be exploited: Rome had no public labour force in anything like sufficient quantity to dispense with contractors. The mines, like public land, became a public source of revenue, farmed out to *publicani*. Again this might well be taken for granted. But again, Tenney Frank advanced an extraordinary view: that the mines were 'directly exploited' by the governor until 179 and only then handed over to *publicani;* and this strange assertion is taken over by his collaborator Van Nostrand in his special treatment of Spain.[19] He bases this almost entirely on the figures given by Livy for precious metals brought back from Spain by various commanders, in which he sees a sudden decrease after 179. This has been rightly disbelieved, though not refuted.[20] But refutation is hardly needed: it is difficult to see where the theory first came from. The figures, as Frank's collaborator sets them out, show what one can only describe as almost random oscillation at all times from their beginning in 206 B.C.[21] In 178 the regular series stops—but not because of any reorganization (none is recorded, or likely): perhaps Livy lost interest, perhaps he changed his source. Livy's reporting of detail is always rather arbitrary, and the argument from silence quite unusable. But it may be that there was simply less fighting, hence fewer takings from it. For the fact is that in 174 Livy again gives figures; but these will not fit Frank's thesis, and therefore have to be arbitrarily 'emended'.[22]

It would be unwise to argue for the accuracy of any particular figure. But the fact—shorn of fanciful interpretation—is that in Livy we have a series of figures purporting to give the amounts of gold and silver brought home by various commanders from Spain between 206 and 178 B.C. There is no mention of their including the profits of mining operations: they are evidently seen by our source as booty, at least to a large extent. Their apparently arbitrary variation can at least to a large extent be correlated with the amount of fighting recorded. After 178, we have only two figures: one for 174, in the usual range, and one for 168, undoubtedly much smaller. Since the income from the mines must have been both large and fairly regular—presumably even increasing, as new mines were opened up—there is not the faintest likelihood that this income was at any stage included, or that it was handed over to the governor, to be regarded as part of his spoils. We do in fact know—whatever had gone before—when at least some of the Spanish mines were organized for the profit of Rome; and quite possibly all of the mines then under Roman control. The elder Cato—that shrewd and implacable businessman—was in fact the first Roman to give the Spanish provinces a proper organization;[23] and as part of this he 'instituted large revenues from iron and silver mines, and after their institution the province became every day more profitable'. So far Livy.[24] Nor do we have to guess at the ultimate source of that clear statement. Of Cato's own history, commonly called *Origines*, only small fragments survive in quotation by other authors. One of them, as it happens, waxes almost lyrical over the wealth of Spain in—iron and silver mines.[25] He adds, in characteristic style and manner: 'There is a mountain of salt: the more you take away from it, the bigger it grows.' Now, we can be quite sure why this mountain of salt attracted the shrewd Cato's attention and what he did with it: we have seen that salt had long been a State monopoly, farmed out to *publicani*. But, remembering the low price of salt, we can understand why later historians did not mention it—as Cato himself had—together with the iron and silver mines. However, we can use it as a safe clue: the iron and silver mines, like the salt, undoubtedly were farmed out to Roman *publicani*. What had been done with them before? We simply do not know. Quite probably nothing. For it had taken the Romans a long time to decide what to do with the Spanish *prouinciae* they had occupied; and once they had decided on permanent occupation, the immediate result was the major revolt that Cato was sent to suppress. There is every reason to believe that the exploitation of the mines, like the administration of the *prouinciae* themselves, had at least not been put on a permanent footing before.[26]

Mining, of course, like the territory under Roman control, was gradually expanded. New mines were opened and exploitation was probably intensified. We have a vivid account in Diodorus, of how at the height of it slaves were literally worked to death as quickly as possible, to produce the maximum of profit in the shortest possible time.[27] It was unskilled work, and it was economically more profitable to replace them than to feed and clothe them for any length of time, especially after their inevitable disablement by the work. This, in fact, is one of the few examples known, of slavery at its theoretical extreme—a spectacle of human beings regarded as expendable objects, such as even rural slavery in the Italian countryside never provided. Strabo, quoting Polybius,[28] gives us more details on the economic (as distinct from the human) side than we usually get on such matters: he claims to give the profits of the enterprise. The silver mines near New Carthage, he says, were fifty Roman miles in circumference—not a very helpful statement, since we do not know their shape! But, to take an average value for the area, we may estimate something over 100 square miles. In Polybius' time, they brought the Roman People 25,000 denarii in revenue per day and employed 40,000 workers. That is an enormous enterprise, by any standards, ancient or modern; and it was just one complex of mines out of many we know of, though obviously, in Polybius' day, the most impressive: we must recall that he visited the area.[29]

Let us again attempt what calculation is possible. The sum—since there were clearly no 'rest days'—comes to about 9 million denarii a year; which (as we can see, now that we are more familiar with the scale of the Roman economy) is a very large sum indeed: we remember the (approximately) $3\frac{1}{2}$ million per year estimated as public booty in a series of profitable wars, and values around 1 million for various army supply contracts. In fact, the sum is so large that we must take the figure (despite Strabo's language: we do not have Polybius' actual text, of course) as referring to output figures, rather than to profit. If this is correct, the value of the enterprise to the Roman economy is much reduced (though still by no means negligible): the contract price could only be a fraction of this figure, in view of the huge investment and overheads of the business, even if profit margins were low.[30] Diodorus tells us that the Spanish mines had long been the foundation of Punic power. If (as is likely) he refers to the period between the two Punic Wars, this may well be true; and it again shows that their contribution to Roman finances was by no means negligible. But again, in view of the size of Roman power in the second century, as compared with that of Carthage at the time indicated, we must beware of exaggerating; and we must set whatever the profits were against the cost—material and moral—of the constant fighting in Spain.

Again, what would be most interesting to us here would be to know the size of the contractors' profits: how tight was supervision, and how much was allowed? But again, we simply do not know. All we can say is that it obviously varied with the censors: this haphazard element was an integral part of the administrative system of the Republic, and everyone learnt to live with it. We have two instances of major trouble between censors and *publicani* in the period we are considering, showing that control could be successfully asserted—but perhaps also that really firm control was exceptional. However, the instances concerned make it amply clear that, whatever the economic benefits reaped by the *publicani*, these were—at this period—not easily translated into political power. The myth of the necessary co-ordination of economic strength with political power—so often proved false in our own day—is totally at variance with the facts of Roman society. We must now proceed to investigate these instances of conflict: often noted, of course, they have not (to my knowledge) been very thoroughly inspected; and they may have something to teach us beyond the facts of the actual struggles.

As might have been expected, the great Cato, as censor (in 184 B.C.) with his colleague and friend L. Valerius Flaccus, tried to clamp down on the profits of private citizens at the expense of the Treasury: his mind was always on money, and—to give him credit—on the public interest. The censors sold the collection of the public revenues at the highest prices, the contracts for goods and services (*ultro tributa*) at the lowest.[31] We can be certain, incidentally, that the Spanish mines would be included in this policy: as we have seen, Cato knew them as well as anyone, and appreciated their earning potential for the State. Next, we are told, the 'prayers and tears' of the afflicted *publicani* moved the Senate to annul the contracts (Plutarch says that it was claimed they allowed no profit), and it ordered the censors to let new ones. But the censors' powers were not to be trifled with: even at the height of the Senate ascendancy, the censors were not the Senate's servants; and Cato was not one to take orders from those who had no right to give them. The censors, naturally, had to comply to the extent of letting new contracts, since these were an essential part of the State machinery. But they first barred the companies that had bought the original contracts from the new sale—an action always within the magistrate's power—and then sold all the contracts at slightly lower prices (*eadem paullum imminutis pretiis*), thus arriving at the same balance for the State. An attempt by Cato's enemies in the Senate to prosecute him—for personal reasons rather than in political support of the *publicani*—came to nothing.[32]

Vague as it is, the report in Livy gives us valuable information. First, there must have been genuine and fierce competition for the contracts; otherwise Cato's prices could not have been obtained. (We must remember that the government, ultimately, depended on the *publicani* for the provision of their essential services.) In particular, even though the Senate had officially disapproved of the prices obtained and annulled the contracts, it seems that Cato and his colleagues had no difficulty in getting a similar balance of prices the second time round, even after the removal of the leading competitor in each case. It is perhaps reassuring to see that normal conditions were very different from what we have noticed in the emergency of the war with Hannibal, when the State had to make major concessions to persuade firms to take on the contracts at all. The incident makes it amply clear that there was no ring or cartel—which entitles us to conclude that, even under censors less strict than Cato, profits would be held down to a level tolerable for the State. The free market may not be a perfect instrument; but it undoubtedly offers certain safeguards, provided there is no combination to nullify it.

We may further deduce that there was not as yet any strict specialization in contract business: genuine competition of the sort we have been able to disengage implies numerous unsuccessful bidders. They must have been prepared, as a matter of course, to turn to other things if the contract did not come their way.[33] We cannot tell whether the associations bidding for the contracts were at this time permanent or—as had apparently been the case in the Hannibalic War—formed *ad hoc*. But in any case, our suspicions of major anachronism when Livy speaks of a 'class' of *publicani* at this time are confirmed. The picture must at least be grossly exaggerated. For there were as yet no full-time specialists in public contracts. Nor can there as yet have been much specialization *within* the field of public contracts. The same companies must have gone in for the tax contracts and the *ultro tributa*, or at least some of each. We recall that, after the official cancellation of all Cato's contracts, as already 'unprofitable', the new contracts were let at lower prices on both sides of the ledger. The censors made no concession (as was to be expected of Cato), but merely paid less for goods and services and took correspondingly less for revenue collection. But how could supply contracts originally 'unprofitable' become profitable enough for the purchasing company by this operation? The answer, of course, is that they could not. We may safely assume slight exaggeration in the tears of the successful bidders trying to make a mockery of the censors' first auction (*ludificari* is Livy's word—possibly ultimately from Cato, who likes words of this type). But at the best, their contracts were only marginally profitable. Lower the price of a marginal contract for *ultro tributa*, and the bidder will inevitably be in the red. In that case, no amount of competition will produce a bidder. On the other hand, with prices for *revenue* contracts also lowered, their terms must have been improved. Why did the careful censor take this step, which *prima facie* was against the interests of the Treasury? Perhaps the answer is now obvious. The only way in which bidders could be obtained on the new terms was for revenue contracts to be linked to contracts for *ultro tributa* (the censors, of course, had full freedom to adapt the terms of their auction), with bidders forced to take both. Since Cato sold his contracts, the step obviously worked. But it shows— as far as we are concerned—that there was as yet no strict specialization within the field of the *publica*: in principle, clearly, the collection of revenues and the furnishing of supplies require different methods and a different organization. But companies were apparently willing to combine the two. Cato's act of conspicuous defiance turns out to be useful to the historian.

The function of the companies as a whole is now also clearer. Whether or not permanently constituted, what they contributed was not organization in the sense of skilled personnel: they did not manufacture togas and tunics, or breed horses; they did not even employ a permanent corps of specialists in revenue collection or the purchase of horses: such large and highly skilled staffs —and we have seen enough about the business to understand that staffs would have to be both large and, at the higher levels, highly skilled—could not be carried by a company that did not succeed in getting a contract; and the evidence for genuine and even fierce competition, at this time, is conclusive. What the companies provided was capital and top management, based on general business experience. As far as permanent staff was concerned, this must have been small in numbers, and able to be used for different kinds of business—revenues or *ultro tributa,* as the case demanded; or, if the bid failed, private business, financial or commercial. In other words, the companies can only have functioned, at this time, by taking over existing substructures and superimposing managing staff. This, of course, can be stated only as a general principle. It was quite likely that a firm specializing (say) in private building—which was also going on at the time, on a lavish scale— would purchase a building contract and be able to employ the whole of its experience and resources on it. Indeed, we may well conjecture that private concerns in similar lines of business would always be among the bidders for public contracts. But the story of Cato's censorship leads us to the conclusion that they were not the only ones, nor perhaps the most important, over the whole field.

As usual, we have no detailed information. We must believe

that there were permanent skilled staffs in each line of public
business—obviously so in the case of the mines, but equally (no
doubt) in the case of revenue collection, or the organization of
the purchase of thousands of tunics from industry which, after
all, was more or less of a 'cottage' type, and their transport to a
remote theatre of war. Once we realize that there was competition
—and this is undeniable—we see that the game would have produced its own rules. The outgoing company, if unsuccessful in
gaining a new contract, would obviously be as glad to dispose of its
specialized substructure as the incoming company was to buy it;
and the rules of the market would produce a fair price, at least
over the whole range of the business. But these are not matters
in which Roman historians showed any interest, and we must
be content with drawing reasonable general conclusions.

The next recorded clash between censors and *publicani* confirms our general impressions and adds further information. Censors were normally elected every five years, and there is no record
of trouble in 179 or 174. The year 179 is specially significant. It
was the end of the period of the second lot of contracts of Cato's
censorship; and no one complained or asked for concessions.
(There can be no doubt that any such request would have brought
Cato into vociferous action.) Moreover, 179 (as we have seen)
is the first recorded occasion of a major grant of revenue for the
purpose of public building: the contracts in that line must have
been larger than usual. For 174 we have no such report; but that
is not evidence for the absence of such a grant, which we pick up
again in 169.[34] Perhaps the censors in those years were less watch-
ful than those of 184; but this is a little unlikely for 179, since that
was a notable censorship, responsible for major administrative
reorganization (including the field of taxation): it is unlikely that
M. Aemilius Lepidus did not keep an experienced and interested
eye on the extensive public contracts he let. The lack of conflict
may perhaps be attributed in part to more diplomatic behaviour
than Cato's; but in part, surely, to the simple fact that the *publicani*,
for the time being, had learnt their lesson. Nothing had been
gained by the attack on Cato and, as we saw, there were no com-
plaints at the end of that *lustrum*. This fact by itself makes it clear
that Cato had won; and his immediate successors no doubt profited. Whether this effect carried on through 174, we cannot know.
But the fact is that that censorship also was peaceful, as far as the
publicani were concerned. And this time we have cause for suspicion.

In 169 B.C. there was more trouble.[35] Tiberius Sempronius Gracchus (father of the tribunician reformers) and C. Claudius Pulcher did not try to avoid it. When they came to let the contracts, no one who had bought any contract in the censorship of 174 was allowed to bid, or even to be associated with a bidding company. What precisely had gone wrong with the previous contracts, we are not told; but it must have been very serious, for the censors to risk extreme unpopularity and worse. Moreover, it is very likely that important individuals who had headed the companies concerned were personally censured and punished. In any case, the men excluded from the bidding complained to the Senate, which (this time) gave them no comfort, but upheld the censors —another sign that the trouble was serious and the censors' action well founded. A tribune named P. Rutilius, who had a personal grievance against the censors, now took up the case of those affected: he proposed a bill to cancel the censors' edict. A really major conflict inevitably developed; the result was that the censors were accused of treason by the tribune and Claudius was barely acquitted by the centuriate assembly. The details do not concern us; but the acquittal meant that the People, like the Senate, had in the end supported the censors, and their edict stood. (They had their revenge by severely punishing the tribune, which no doubt finally confirmed the unquestioned authority of the censors.)[36]

We cannot tell what was the serious trouble that had developed over the contracts of 174. Livy's silence is excruciating. That it was serious is, as we saw, undeniable. We can only note the vast expansion in the whole business of public contracting that had been produced by the two preceding censorships (of 179 and 174). The censors of 179 had transformed the tax structure, and we shall have more to say about this. The censors of 174 had not only been active in building in the city, but for the first time had let major building contracts throughout the Roman parts of Italy.[37] Moreover, one of the censors of 174 was a very unsatisfactory character, Q. Fulvius Flaccus.[38] The revision of the tax system and the introduction of a grant of 20 per cent of the total revenue for public building may well have reduced genuine competition (at least temporarily) and produced a crop of speculators in the contracting business: the usual effects of excessively rapid expansion in any part of the economy. It is not surprising that trouble should have developed precisely at this time. However, the important fact that we do know is that the censors of 169 were severe in repressing it, and that Senate and People supported them. And this although one of the censors is reported to have been personally arrogant and unpopular, which makes their success before the People even more impressive and more decisive. Had it not been for this unpopularity, and the accident that one of the tribunes had a personal axe to grind, there would obviously have been no serious challenge to the censors at all: unlike Cato, they had the Senate behind them. The impression we gain is that, in spite of the enormous sums that passed through their hands, the *publicani,* on the whole, were still firmly under public control. Though in favourable circumstances they could exert some pressure, they were not an established pressure group able to wield political power of their own.

The two instances of conflict with the censors show us why this was so. In the first place, we must note the simple fact of the free market and competition. As long as there was this element, profits would be kept down, provided the censors were honest and knew their job. (And it was to be presumed that normally this would be so.) Cato's success had shown that, in the last resort, a boycott of the contract auctions could not be organized: the *publicani* lacked the only really effective weapon they might have used. Moreover, in both cases—and especially in the second—we see the effects of the solidarity of the Senate. In the case of Cato, a faction of personal enemies (he was a man who gloried in his *inimicitiae*) had succeeded in bringing about the cancellation of the first contracts; but when the censors persevered, and particularly when there was a danger of their authority being challenged by prosecution, the Senate rallied to support them. In the second case, support was prompt and unanimous; and the *auctoritas* of this support sufficed to rally the People.

Nevertheless, the affair of 169 was taken very seriously by the Senate: it had been a near thing, in the Assembly. When the war in Macedonia ended, the country was not annexed, even though it had become clear that it was not safe to leave the royal dynasty in power. The result was a very unsatisfactory arrangement: a division of the country into four 'free' republics, tributary to Rome and restricted in various ways.[39] One result of this was that the Roman exchequer denied itself the profit from *portoria* (customs dues) collected in that country—and denied the *publicani* the chance of collecting them. But there was more striking self-denial. The King's lands and the mines (which had been royal property) might have been taken over by the victorious

Romans as the King's successors. They were not, and the mines, in fact, were closed down. Similarly, the huge forests of excellent shipbuilding timber, also a royal preserve, were apparently not to be exploited. That this action was directed against the *publicani* is explicitly stated in our source[40] and we have no right to deny it.[41]

The amount of the revenue of which the Romans thereby deprived themselves must be fully realized, for the importance of this step to be understood. The sum found by L. Paullus in the royal treasuries of Macedon is reliably reported[42] as over 6,000 talents (i.e. 36 million denarii, at the conventional rate of conversion), in actual cash and metal. As Livy himself points out,[43] it is remarkable that such a sum was accumulated in thirty years from a major war lost to the Romans,[44] and after five years of a new war that had itself inevitably been expensive: Livy's source thought it had cost as much again (though we do not have the figure that source gave for what Paullus actually found). As Livy implies, the royal mines provided the major part of that revenue, with the other royal possessions accounting for most of the rest. At a conservative estimate for the cost of the war, at least 50 million denarii must have been accumulated over those thirty years; i.e., the Romans voluntarily deprived themselves of revenues that must have amounted to between 1 and 2 million denarii per year, less the tribute they imposed. Though there are too many gaps in our knowledge to give us anything approaching an accurate estimate, it is clear that the loss was considerable. The tribute that the kings had received was halved.

It is strange to find the Senate so concerned for the welfare of a defeated enemy population as to incur such losses; indeed, it is the only such case that I recall.[45] We must accept the statement that it was done to avoid the introduction of Roman *publicani*— if only because it is hard to think of another plausible reason. But the pure altruism is a little too good to ring true. In the light of this study, it is easy to see that the Senate's action must be connected with the conflict of 169. Obviously, the Senate was aware of political danger, despite its final victory in that struggle. Not only was there the fact that the *publicani* of the previous quinquennium had seriously misbehaved—Cato had shown that this could be dealt with. There was worse: they had in fact come within an ace of convicting a censor in office. Indeed, this was the nearest any censor in Roman history ever came to being condemned. Only eight centuries had saved C. Claudius.

But worse still: out of the eighteen privileged centuries of *equites* —the officer class, including senators and their relatives and usually the most reliable element of the assembly—eight had certainly voted against him. (We do not know the rest.) So had many centuries of the first class. We have noted the fact that, as far back as the Hannibalic War, the leading *publicani* belonged to the 'equestrian' class; though there had never been any suggestion that they dominated it. In his account of the events of 169, Livy explicitly asserts the connection, claiming that the censors' action against the equestrian class as a whole was connected with their action against the *publicani* in giving offence to the same people.[46] It could no doubt be argued that this might still be rewriting in the late Republic. However, we are now in the full light of history, when men like Cato were recording the events of their own day; moreover, we still have to explain the Senate's action in Macedonia: what was the danger the Senate saw in the *publicani,* which it paid such a high price to avert?[47] The obvious answer is that the Senate was losing the support of the substratum of its own class: the *publicani* were gaining excessive influence in the equestrian order. The very choice of charge and assembly, on the part of the tribune P. Rutilius, is significant, and bears out Livy's interpretation in the respects we have noted. Giving up the possibility of impeachment before the assembly in which he could preside and which was—by Roman standards—much more democratic, he chose to prosecute in the centuriate assembly, in which he had no particular privileges and where the votes were heavily weighted in favour of the wealthiest class. The details that Livy gives us about the voting explain and justify the choice. They also show the seriousness of the blow to the Senate's prestige, on which its power was based.

The insubordination of an odd member of the senatorial class was a phenomenon familiar in Roman politics: the oligarchy as a whole was strong enough to live with it, just as modern Western societies have, on the whole, been able to live with a high level of vocal opposition and disobedience. But a large-scale undermining of the loyalty of the upper class had never happened before. It was nothing less than concern over the basis of the Senate's rule—rule by respect and consent, based above all on the support of the non-political members of its own class—that inspired the Senate's fear, and (we may now add) its action over Macedonia in 167, when the events of the censorship of 169 were still a vivid memory. One would like to know the effect of this on the next censorship, in 164. Unfortunately Livy's text has by then failed us and we have no political details; though, strangely enough—in view of the absence of our main source and the general paucity of information on Roman politics at this time—special mildness towards the *equites* is attested.[48] This may not be due entirely to the personalities of the particular censors (though the difference that this could make is well attested). It fits in with the well-known Roman principle of *parcere subiectis*: to crush opposition and then be mild to the vanquished had for generations been proclaimed as a principle of policy.

Let us, for the moment, return to a somewhat earlier period. We can perhaps find confirmation of the improvement in the political position of the *publicani*. As we have mentioned, the revenue from public land was among those farmed out to them in each censorship. Before the Hannibalic War it had not been a very important item. After victory, this suddenly changed. Vast tracts of land belonging to rebellious allies (particularly in the south of Italy) were confiscated, and *ager publicus* suddenly became (at least potentially) a major source of revenue to the State. It was not exploited as such. In 196 and again in 193, exceptionally active aediles convicted many who were guilty of grazing offences.[49] The penalties imposed were considerable. But it may be assumed that such vigour was exceptional: Livy singles it out for mention. This would hardly be because the offence as such was rare. In 173 a consul was entrusted with the odd task of going to the most valuable part of the public land—the land of Capua, all of which had been expropriated as a punishment for the city's rebellion and only a small part of which had been sold off[50]—and there seeing to the proper demarcation of the property of the Roman People, which had been seriously encroached upon by private individuals. It took a consul to attempt this: that shows the seriousness of the task, and its difficulty. In the following year a tribune passed a law, resulting from the consul's investigations, ordering future censors to farm out the revenues of this highly profitable territory.[51] Livy himself draws the obvious conclusion that this had not been done in all the years (nearly forty) since the confiscation, to the great benefit of eminent individuals. It was this official negligence—failure to demarcate and failure to collect rent—that had been responsible for what (to judge by the consul's mission) must have been extensive encroachment and the establishment of powerful private interests. It is further evidence for the political impotence of the *publicani* that, in all these years, they had not been able to secure the contracts for farming this land, to which they were legally entitled.[52] The fact that, just after the censorship of 174, this overdue step was at last taken, although it may mean no more than that the Senate had decided that this revenue could no longer be spared,[53] is very probably to be taken (at least in part) together with our other evidence for an increase in pressure on the part of the *publicani,* four years before their major conflict with the censors and the Senate.

About the same time—almost certainly between 172 and 167—a law was passed limiting occupation of public land by one individual to about 300 acres. This, as we happen to know, was unwelcome to a large number of senators, who no doubt occupied large stretches of such land.[54] And since, at this time, there is no evidence for concern with the welfare of the peasantry or with increasing its numbers, a very plausible conclusion is that the chief purpose of this law was to prevent the accumulation of large tracts of public land in the hands of men too powerful to be forced to pay for it: the tax-collector always prefers the small man.

To sum up: we may say that there is good evidence of an increase in the power of the *publicani* around 170 B.C.—no doubt in part the result of vastly increased economic opportunities that had come with the great wars and the new uses found for public money; but, we must add, in part also the result of the fact that a major war—the war against Perseus—was going on at the time and had in fact been foreseen as early as 173. We have had occasion to note that the emergency produced by a war strengthened the hands of the contractors, making the government more dependent on their services and—by expanding the range of contracts—reducing competition at the auctions. A serious situation revealed in 169 (and we may voice a suspicion, which unfortunately cannot be supported by evidence except to recall the events of the Hannibalic war, that there had *inter alia* been a major scandal connected with military supplies) led to severe action against the *publicani* by the censors, with the full support of the Senate; and the resulting trial of strength, though it ended with the defeat of the *publicani,* sufficiently worried the Senate to induce it to forgo most of the revenues of Macedonia. It is not altogether unexpected that this situation did not last long. The censors of 164 helped to secure a reconciliation; and in 158 the royal mines —and probably the other royal properties, though our evidence does not explicitly state it[55]—were reopened and duly farmed out to *publicani.* The date probably means—though again, we cannot tell, owing to the loss of Livy—that the censors of 159/8 were the ones who decided to take this step. The difficulties between the Senate and the contractors were gradually being resolved—partly, no doubt, as earlier in the case of Cato, by the reaffirmation of the Senate's power; but, of course, it was in any case in the long run far more profitable for both parties to work in harmony than to suffer loss of income and services through conflict. By the middle of the century, it seems, the system had adjusted itself and, on its new and much larger scale, was again working to the general satisfaction.

It is just about this time[56] that we have valuable evidence on both the importance of the contractors' operations and the limitation of their power. This comes in the famous passage of Polybius[57] in which he sets out the working of the 'balanced' Roman constitution, showing how each part of the state and of society is dependent on all others. The passage of interest to us is worth quoting: 'The People is dependent on the Senate and has to court the Senate's good will . . .; for numerous contracts—too numerous to count—are placed by the censors for the building and repair of public works throughout Italy; and besides there are rivers, harbours, parks, mines, lands—in fact everything that is Roman public property. Now all these are actually handled by the People, and there is hardly anyone who is not involved either in the sale of these contracts or in the kinds of business to which they give rise. Some buy the contracts in person from the censors; some become partners of the purchasers; others stand surety or pledge their own property on their behalf. And all this is decided by the Senate.' After mentioning the Senate's power to grant dispensations and deal with lawsuits arising out of these contracts, he concludes: 'So all are in the *fides* of the Senate.'

It is generally recognized[58] that Polybius is here—anachronistically, since he claims to be describing the situation as it was at the beginning of the Hannibalic War!—in fact dealing with the state of affairs that he himself knew, around 150 B.C. It is also quite clear, and widely noticed,[59] that he is *chiefly* interested in the *publicani* when he speaks about the People; indeed, an eminent modern historian waxes eloquently sarcastic over this: applying Polybius' statement to the small peasant in danger of losing his farm, Toynbee says: 'The suggestion that he disposed of spare money for investment in public contracts would have been taken by him to be a joke, and a bad joke, at his expense.'[60]

It is easy to reverse the verdict of the skilled and conscientious contemporary observer, from the vantage point of the almost total loss of the relevant evidence. Of course, Polybius—like all of us —may be wrong; but he will have to be *proved* wrong before this is stated as a fact, and before he is held up to ridicule. Admittedly, Polybius' chief interest is in men wealthy enough to invest in the companies of public contractors. We may safely allow that ownership of shares in these companies was indeed widely distributed— more widely than modern prejudice is willing to recognize; even though the peasant in danger of losing his farm may possibly not have owned any. (But do we know even this?) However, Polybius is writing as a political historian. As such, he is surely right to be interested in those who were wealthy enough—and, as they had at times shown, determined enough—to try to challenge the Senate's power. Our 'age of the common man' has developed a praiseworthy interest in the oppressed masses: there is every reason—as far as our evidence permits it—to attend to them. But the fact remains that, at this time, they played no real part in Roman politics. Polybius is rightly concerned with the politically active elements, since he is writing about the balance of political power. Had he written a century later, much of what he wrote would have been different, and possibly this also. His critics would do well to learn from him.

Polybius was writing political history, and writing under the impact of the conflicts of the 160s, most of which he had been able to observe, while we can only conjecture them from scattered and defective evidence. But he was nevertheless not totally unaware of the non-political masses. For he distinguishes between the actual sale of the contracts and the 'business arising out of them'.[61] The latter, surely, is a valid point, which modern writers who claim an interest in economic developments ought to remember. Not unexpectedly, it has been persuasively argued by a modern scholar not concerned with Polybius or the *publicani*, but with the economic developments that produced the crisis which the Gracchi tried to remedy, that the vast increase in building and other public works, not only in Rome, but to some extent in cities throughout Italy, led to an economic boom, in which Toynbee's poor peasant who lost his land found ready employment—unless, indeed, he actually preferred to give up his small holding and go to the city to profit by the new opportunities.[62] The freedman working as a revenue collector or in a clothing 'factory' or in the building trade; the small employer for whom a few slaves spun cloth; the innkeeper or the producer of earthenware containers—they all, in a very real sense, depended on 'the business arising out of' the public contracts. While, as we all know, a slow agricultural revolution was going on in Italy, with cash crops and larger estates taking the place—though perhaps to a more limited extent than has sometimes been claimed—of small-scale cereal production at subsistence level, it was to a large extent the business arising out of the public contracts, increasingly pervading the economic life of Rome and of Roman Italy, that helped and even invited the victims of the agricultural changes to readjust themselves to new conditions and find a living in the cities. And it was the fading away of some of the public activity after the middle of the century that intensified and made acute and threatening—though it did not, of course, by itself produce—the crisis that faced Rome in 133 B.C.

All this is an important part of the history of the *publicani,* and Polybius knew it.

III

The Rise to Power

We have seen what large sums were passing through the hands of the public companies in the first half of the second century B.C. and have noted signs of an increase in their power after a generation of this. They could at times find allies in the Senate, using the personal and factional antagonisms within it for their advantage; and they could even find a tribune to become their champion, despite the unanimous disapproval of the Senate: we remember, by contrast, how at the height of the Hannibalic War a tribune actually related to a *publicanus* under attack had not dared to help him. But we have also seen the obvious limits of their power. In their conflict with the censors and the Senate they had in fact always been unsuccessful in the end; the tribune who had taken up their case in 169 had ruined his own career; and this whole affair, followed by the Senate's action in Macedonia, had shown who was master in the state. By the middle of the century this was realized: Polybius had no doubt that the *publicani* were in the *fides* of the Senate; and he was a shrewd observer of contemporary politics and did not underestimate the extent of their economic activity and importance.

Moreover, they seem to be personally free from political ambition. It might be said: perhaps of necessity. It must have been

easy enough for a prominent *publicanus,* then as later, to enter
the lower reaches of the Senate: perhaps their supporter P. Rutilius
had risen from their ranks (though no one alleges this). But for
real eminence one needed at least a solid land-owning background.
M. Cato, with this background and the support of a Patrician
Valerius Flaccus, had no real difficulty in rising to the top. The
first attested consul from the ranks of the *publicani* is P. Rupilius,
whose success was due to the personal friendship and support of
P. Scipio Aemilianus. His origins were remembered against him,[1]
even though he became consul and his daughter married a Patrician Fabius Maximus. His brother, supported by Scipio and by
Publius himself, failed to reach the consulship—which is said to
have broken Publius' heart, so that he died of grief.[2]

Frank suggests[3] that what prevented the *publicani* from advanc-
ing to the highest posts in the state, in spite of their enormous
economic power, was their suffering under the proscriptions of
L. Sulla. That is an odd argument, even for one who underesti-
mates their economic importance in the first half of the second
century: by Sulla's day they should have had plenty of time to
get there. Toynbee, rightly rejecting this suggestion, says that the
obstacle was 'political';[4] and in some sense of that word this is
undoubtedly true—indeed, a truism. But Toynbee seems to take
it in the wrong sense. He fails to observe that, ever since the days
of the Hannibalic War when we first have concrete evidence on
them (and therefore, quite possibly, for a long time before that),
the senior and most important of the *publicani* had come from the
governing class itself: they were *equites,* fellow members of what
one may call the officer class, related (in known cases) to senators
and magistrates. If they were excluded from the highest power, it
was not through unwillingness to broaden the basis of the governing class.

There was certainly social prejudice, and that is more important.
Rome was not a plutocracy pure and simple: wealth was not
enough, though it was required. Toynbee reverts to what one had
hoped was a view long overcome in scholarly circles: of a 'middle
class' of businessmen[5] knocking imperiously at the doors of power
and kept out by a landed aristocracy narrow-mindedly defending its
political privilege. The picture may be appropriate for eighteenth-
century Europe, whose spirit is more familiar to that great
scholar than that of the Roman Republic. In Rome, at the time
with which we are dealing, there is no unsuccessful attempt by a
business class to gain political power—there is, to be brief, no

such attempt at all; perhaps even no such class at all. The businessman knows his place in the order of things, whether he be *publicanus* or private *negotiator*. He has no interest in government.
And the governing aristocracy, while unwilling to admit too many
of its own members to the circle of the nobility—i.e., for practical
purposes, to the consulate—was always ready and sometimes even
eager to admit chosen members of the *equites* to lower office: they,
after all, were of the same class (for members of the Senate were
themselves *equites*)—the officer class, as we have called it, distinguished from the rank and file by the 'public horse' conferred by
the censors.[6] This class traditionally furnished recruits to the
Senate, promoted by patrons inside it.[7] This was how Cato and
Marius—to mention the most eminent—rose to power, and there
were many like them in the lower reaches of the Senate. Rome
was by no means a caste society. But it was an aristocratic and
highly stratified society, with social mobility kept down to a slow
rate and with landed property socially required for membership
of the governing class; and within the governing class, those who
seemed exalted when seen from below had, on the whole, still a
very long way to go before they attained real power and political
importance.

Landed property was the basis of membership of the upper
class—on the whole, the basis of 'equestrian' wealth as of senatorial;[8] and below the august ranks of the officer class as a whole,
the basis of municipal eminence. By law and tradition, senators
had long been forbidden to engage in commerce or to take part
in the purchase of public contracts. They formed the political
part of the upper class. Those members of the officer class who
had no political ambitions were free to engage in such activities—
with the result that they became their most important practitioners,
on account of their very eminence of social rank. But those whose
fortunes were largely derived from this sort of activity—even if
their land-owning background was unquestioned—were regarded
as unfit for political office, and even more so for political advancement. Merchants—not to mention *publicani*—might, as Cicero was
to say,[9] retire from their trade and invest their money in respectable Italian land. They would then be socially accepted. But they
might still be regarded as not quite fit to be senators, certainly
not to be consuls; though their sons probably found full acceptance easier. The families of lesser (non-equestrian) *publicani*, like
those of merchants, must often have risen to acceptance into the
upper class in this way, slow and arduous though it was: we must

remember that at this time there appears to have been no specialization in *publica* as distinct from other forms of business activity.

But, to return to where we started: the senior among the *publicani* were already *equites,* already had the required background. They, however, lost their qualification for governing by taking up that form of business. P. Rupilius was a member of an eminent family in the important Latin city of Praeneste—solidly endowed, one would think. Yet he was despised as a *publicanus.* The very fact that such men might gain great wealth by means not open to their peers would no doubt increase resentment. Social superiority had to be asserted, in compensation. C. Marius, we are told,[10] was slighted by his noble commander Q. Metellus because 'it appeared that he had been a *publicanus*'. Marius' credentials as a member of the officer class were unimpeachable: his family belonged to the municipal aristocracy of Arpinum (though we cannot tell how long it had done so), and he had served his military apprenticeship under P. Scipio Aemilianus, with great distinction and in the personal suite of the commander.[11] And the charge may not even be true: certainly Cicero, who—on many public occasions—would not have thought it a matter of reproach, never mentions any such activity by Marius. However, whether true or not, the charge was apparently made; and that is interesting in itself. The prejudice that kept the *publicani* out of government, even though by birth and rank the more eminent of them seemed fully qualified for it, was basically social. But there is no reason to think that, on the whole, it was resented. Nothing in our sources gives us any reason to depict—as Toynbee does—the class of *publicani,* or businessmen on the whole, as one straining at the leash, eager to be allowed into high office and resentful at being kept out. There were ambitious men, like Marius and the Rupilii. They, as we have seen, were men who did not so much want to rise as not to admit that they had fallen. But the actual quarrels between *publicani* and the Senate were, as we saw and shall see again, not over access to office: they were strictly over the terms of the contracts. Businessmen wanted to get on with their business, under the protection of government.

The prejudice felt by the ruling aristocracy against wealth acquired in business—even by members of its own class—is obvious and may not be denied. But human motives are never wholly simple. It should be clear that there was a good case, in equity and in political theory, for excluding *publicani* from political power. Polybius in fact implies it, and there is no reason to doubt that by his day eminent Romans were aware of it. It was the task of government to govern, in the strict sense of the term —not to engage in business. *Public* business, in particular, had to be under the supervision of the Senate and magistrates; hence it had to be divorced from it, and its practitioners could not themselves take part in that supervision, any more than senators could be allowed to take part in that business. There have been many states run by a business aristocracy; but Rome was not one of them. Nor were there even the subterfuges that we ourselves permit. The convention that, today, allows an eminent business-man to accept a position in the government, provided he goes through the ritual of resigning his director's post and putting his shares in trust, would have been rejected as hypocritical by most second-century Romans—had they ever thought of it. The *publicanus,* with his special interests, could not be expected to be unprejudiced in governing. If this, to some extent, was rationaliza-tion of prejudice, as we have admitted, it is important to realize that it nevertheless had a more solid base as well—a view of the functions of government that (in the ancient context, in particular) was far from indefensible. Each age has its own conventions, moral and social, often rooted in prejudice and—across the centuries—easily seen as dishonourable. They can nevertheless be sincerely believed in, and contain an element of reason.

In fact, landed property could be felt to be above influencing political decisions, in a sense in which trade (not to mention public contracts) would not be. Universally taken for granted by the upper class, it was beyond critical assessment; just as the Found-ing Fathers of the American Republic, speaking of equal rights and freedom from tyranny, could take not only a certain social status, but a certain skin colour, entirely for granted, as beyond discussion, because it was common to them and their circle and thus unnoticed. This is not to say that abuse of one's landed interest was not recognized as dishonourable: the case of the censor who caused a dam to be built in an area where he had large properties aroused attention.[12] But it did not lead people to question what we might call the political neutrality of landed property as such—the accepted fact that it stood above political discussion, since it was (as an institution) common to all who engaged in such discussion. It is not the historian's task to *defend* this view: we see only too clearly how the landed interest of the upper class helped to prevent necessary reform and to plunge the

Republic into the Gracchan crisis. But the historian must try to understand the presuppositions and prejudices of the age he is studying no less than those of his own age, before he attempts a judgment. If he refuses to do so, he is reduced to the ranks of those who have no standard of judgment but their own—individual or collective—prejudices.

This has not been an irrelevant digression. For it has led us to the basic issue from which the Roman political crisis developed and which brought the *publicani* into their relatively brief period of political prominence: the landed interest that was basic to the Roman governing class. We must now see how the challenge to it came about.

We have commented briefly on the agricultural developments in Italy in the second century and on the influx of peasants—dispossessed or merely trying to improve their lot—into the cities and especially into Rome. In all this, as we saw, the *publicani* and the public contracts played a major part; and Polybius shows that men were at least dimly aware of it.[13] We cannot be sure how much building and other public economic activity there was after 167, since we lose the guidance of Livy. But it can be shown that there was still quite an amount, at least at times. In 146 B.C. both Carthage and Corinth were destroyed. We do not know the figures for booty captured;[14] but there was certainly another major infusion into the Roman economy, and the effects seem to have been very similar to those earlier in the century. It was soon after this that the Marcian aqueduct was built, at a cost of 45 million denarii:[15] a sign of how many people had flocked into Rome and of how much money there was to cope with the influx. The censorship of 142 was a specially lavish one, which saw, among other works, the gilding of the ornamental ceiling of the Capitoline temple and the building of the Aemilian Bridge, the former undertaken by the conqueror of Corinth and the latter by the conqueror of Carthage.[16] But a few years after this, all this activity ceased.[17] The booty had run out, and only an unpopular guerrilla war in Spain remained, soon joined by a dangerous slave war in Sicily. It is interesting that we nowhere hear of any political part played in all this by the *publicani*: they continued to organize what was required; but they are not recorded either as promoting all the economic activity or as protesting at its cessation. It shows that they still have no thought of political influence as such—influence on the making of policy decisions, as distinct from the limited decisions on actual contracts; and if there were any quarrels even over decisions of the latter type, they are not attested.

It was against the background of economic recession and of difficult and widely disliked wars in Spain and Sicily—the latter particularly menacing both because of the danger of spreading slave unrest and because of the immediate effect of cutting down grain imports for the city of Rome—that Tiberius Gracchus, in 133, proposed his law to enforce the legal limits on the holding of public land and to redistribute the surplus that would become available to the Roman poor. The idea was not his alone: he was supported by some of the leading senators of the day. Both his motives and theirs have been discussed innumerable times, and though the story has a perennial interest—from the historiographic no less than from the strictly historical point of view—it is not my task to tell it here. What does concern us is that it was the unintended effect of this law to call into question the whole aristocratic Roman conception of the state, based as it was on the postulate that landed property made a governing class peculiarly suited for governing and unprejudiced in its approach to public problems. The personal interest in public land that was shared by the whole upper class—senators and *equites*—first frustrated Tiberius' reform and drove him into patent illegality in order to accomplish it, and then killed him for this.[18] None of this was, as Toynbee would have it, the result of a business class's demanding access to positions of power and executive authority; indeed, it is difficult to see how a picture so remote from reality could ever have been advanced in a scholarly work.

The result of the promise and the failure of Tiberius Gracchus was, by striking at the foundations of the Roman polity, to bring out into the open and to sharpen differences of interest that had hitherto been latent and harmless; and in the long run to politicize them and arm them—as Gaius Gracchus was to say—against each other; and hence against the Republic, which depended, as any ordered society does, on the subordination of conflicting interests to a whole, which must be basically the interest of the governing class. The dominant ancient view—recently restated by R. E. Smith[19]—was that it was the Gracchi who destroyed the *concordia* on which the Classical Republic rested. This view, though in many of its aspects oversimplified (as has frequently been shown), contains an essential truth, which is worth restating—provided it is not exaggerated into making the Gracchi morally responsible for the fall of the Republic; it is in no way disproved, as some of Smith's critics tried to disprove it, by attempts—in themselves both justified and important, of course—to explore and to stress the earlier existence of problems, tensions and interest groups. The fate of Tiberius Gracchus exposed the falsity of the basic premiss of the Republican political structure.

The interest groups that now emerge and gain occasional or even permanent cohesion and militancy are far too complex to be subsumed under any simple concept of 'class struggle' as proposed by Toynbee and by some Marxist scholars. Urban poor and rural poor; slaves, freedmen, and free-born; citizens, Latins, and Italians; upper class and lower class; senators and *equites*; landed and financial plutocracy; nobles and mere senators; and, of course, as always, the 'generation gap', which our generation did not invent, but which in every crisis propels impatient and ambitious youth into exciting solutions, pressed with an ardour unaware of problems that will have to be faced—no historian, not even Mommsen (whose view was a particularly simplistic one, akin to Toynbee's), has yet done justice to the whole of this theme: the history of the decline and fall of the Roman Republic still remains to be written, by a sensitive and well-informed historian with no other purpose in mind. Most of us can only follow one or two threads of the web; which is reasonable and useful, provided we do not claim that we have found 'the answer'.

Unfortunately the evidence is often very inadequate, even as regards major developments. Our sources, before Cicero's works become available on contemporary issues, tend to concentrate on the striking and the dramatic—on sedition, violence, and death; and later reinterpretation, for propagandist purposes, can obscure and falsify even what little we have, taking in the modern historian, where the prejudices approach his own.

The problem first arises over the legislation that Tiberius Gracchus is said by Plutarch[20] to have planned when he found he needed a second tribunate in order to pursue his plans. Pliny and Dio[21] imply the same account: the latter goes so far as to say explicitly that Tiberius wanted to transfer the law-courts from the Senate to the *equites*. The best-informed sources—Appian and Cicero—never refer to this. Attributed statements of unfulfilled plans must be suspect in any case; in this case all the more so, as much of the information on Tiberius that Plutarch collected may be derived from a political pamphlet written by his brother Gaius a few years later;[22] claiming to be carrying on his brother's work, Gaius remodelled his brother in his own image.[23] How-

ever, that the idea of 'throwing knives into the forum' was born
in Gracchan circles, and born long before it reached maturity
with Gaius' programme, can be regarded as certain. In Cicero's
dialogue *On the Republic*[24] we have the famous reference to a
law 'on the return of (public) horses', said to be then under discussion and strongly condemned by the chief speaker, P. Scipio
Aemilianus, as a 'new kind of bribery' (*noua largitio*). This has,
ever since Niebuhr, been correctly interpreted as referring to a law
—not otherwise attested, but certainly in force in the late Republic
—under which a man attaining a seat in the Senate (or perhaps
a magistracy of a certain standing) had to return his public horse
at the next census and thus leave the order of *equites,* to which
senators had earlier continued to belong. The dramatic date of the
dialogue is not in doubt: it is set at the time of the Latin Festival
in 129 B.C., a few days—Cicero elsewhere tells us—before Scipio's
death.[25] We know how carefully Cicero researched the historical
background of his dialogues, guarding against any anachronism and
calling on the resources (as well as the actual knowledge) of his
friend Atticus for scholarly assistance.[26] We may therefore take it
as certain that the law concerned had not yet been passed early
in 129: Scipio's condemnation would have been much more
powerful, had it been directed against the effective law rather than
against the proposal, and Cicero must have known that this could
not be done. When was the law passed? It has been usual to
regard it as passed soon after Scipio's death—almost certainly in
129, since there was still plenty of time left in that year. Despite
recent doubts,[27] this still seems the only possible date. Roman
laws did not normally remain subjects of discussion for years,
and both Cicero and his readers knew this. A proposal of this
nature would be made by a tribune and either passed or rejected
in the same year: the very nature of the annual magistracy
ensured this. There can be no real doubt that Cicero had evidence
(probably taken from the law itself, which could be inspected and
which would carry its precise date in its prescript) on the actual
day (not to mention the year) when this law was passed: since
it was a law still in effect in his day, not much care—far less than
is attested in his researches—would have been needed to elicit this
information. Had it been a law passed in (say) 122, seven years
after Scipio's death, it is inconceivable that, without any excuse,
he should have pretended that it was being discussed as early as
that. After all, Scipio (as far as we can tell) does not know about
the plan to deprive the Senate of control of the juries or the plan

to enfranchise the allies; and the latter, at least, would have been highly relevant to some comments he makes, and was in fact proposed as early as 126. It is, of course, theoretically possible that the proposal was made and rejected in 129 (which, from our present point of view, would make little difference) and successfully revived later. But this complicated hypothesis will need positive support, if it is to be preferred to the simpler alternative; and above all, it would have to be explained what Cicero's evidence was for the appearance of the proposal at that time, and its rejection. Clearly, this was at least not a well-known incident, comparable to the struggles over the Gracchan laws; for no certain reference to it has survived. We must, I think, be content with the obvious and assume that the law was both proposed and—in spite of some opposition from eminent senators—passed in 129, its passage falling in the later part of the year, after Scipio's death.

Elsewhere in what has survived of the same dialogue, Cicero mentions the political crisis in Rome: indeed, this is his main reason for choosing the dramatic date as he did.[28] In particular, we know that there had been a split in the Senate itself over the way in which Tiberius had been killed (even though, as usual, the opposition later rallied to defend what had been done);[29] and the agrarian commission that Tiberius had created, and staffed with his followers, continued after his death and remained a focus for discontent and resentment.[30] The events of 133 had made it clear that, despite much sympathy from eminent men, the Senate as a whole could not be persuaded to support reform. If it was to continue as Tiberius had intended and the agrarian commission was now trying to ensure that it should, other allies would have to be found. The lesson was reinforced by the events of 129 itself: it was in that year that P. Scipio Aemilianus paralysed the commission by removing all or most of its judicial powers.[31] We need not be surprised that within a short time of that blow, the new law (of which Scipio so strongly disapproved) was being promoted. The lesson of 133 had been driven home by Scipio himself, and it was bound to be learnt.

The idea was apparently that later refined by C. Gracchus: to drive a permanent wedge into the governing class and split it along the one line of fissure that could be discerned. What had happened —uniquely, as far as we know—in 169, when the voters of the officer class had turned against the *auctoritas* of the Senate, was to be encouraged and institutionalized. A new class was to be created.

As we have seen, the officer class (*equites*) was basically of homogeneous background. When Tiberius had attacked their land-holdings, they had stood together against him. Yet there was a potential difference within that class that might be exploited: the conflicts over the public contracts showed the way. But the pre-requisite was that the non-political element should be given a corporate identity of its own, detached from the ruling circle. This, obviously, was the purpose of the new 'bribe'—the law excluding senators from the (new) officer class. There is another measure of the passing of which we are not informed: that conferring on these same *equites* (as distinct from senators) the privilege of an allocation of fourteen rows of seats at the games.[32] It has some-times been thought that this law should be part of C. Gracchus' legislation; and indeed, it might fit in there. But that legislation is amply reported, with special emphasis on the measures to divide the upper class against itself; it would be strange if one of the most important of those measures—in that it created a visible and indeed conspicuous difference—had been ignored by the whole of our tradition. On the other hand, since the law must certainly have been passed some time in the second century, it seems obvious to link it with the law on the return of the public horse: both measures were intended to set up a new equestrian class and distinguish it from that of the Senate. They obviously belong together, and it is not too hazardous—though one cannot be cer-tain—to suggest that they were both passed in the same year 129, both (since we do not hear about their passing) without effective opposition.[33]

Whatever the truth about the unfulfilled intentions of Tiberius Gracchus, and in particular that of depriving the Senate of its monopoly of the jury court, it is certain that the idea of giving the *equites* a conspicuous corporate identity, as a counterweight to the Senate, arose out of the crisis of 133 and was perfected after Scipio's intervention against the commission in 129. It took the commission a little longer to deal with the substantive injustice that Scipio had seized on in order to pass his measure: the com-plaints of the Italians—whom there is no real evidence that Tiberius had seriously considered—about their helplessness against the commission, and about their having to pay the price for the solution of Rome's problems.[34] The *largitio* in their case—that they should be given the Roman citizenship if they wanted it—was only presented by 126; no doubt the matter had to be discussed with their leaders before action was taken in Rome. The laws about the *equites* had been planned ever since 133 and were now ready to pass. But both plans were a direct consequence of the opposition to Tiberius Gracchus. It is interesting that the two plans are parallel also in creating wants that had not been strongly felt: in the case of the Italians this is clear from the fact that an alternative giving them the right to appeal to the Roman People against acts of Roman magistrates was included, for those who did not want Roman citizenship (thirty years later there is no sign of that); in the case of the *equites* we have already seen that there is no evidence of an antecedent demand for political status. Of course, in both cases there will have been individuals who expressed such a desire: this will be how the ideas first occurred to the politicians who formulated them. And the interest groups concerned certainly existed and did not have to be created. But as political issues, both the equestrian order and the problem of allied citizenship spring directly out of the Gracchan experience: it was the action of Gracchan politicians that gave political consciousness and political aims to these two groups.[35]

The idea—attributed to Tiberius Gracchus, as we saw—of giving the new equestrian class some public function in the trial of senators belongs to the same political circles. Though the fact that it was brought up only by C. Gracchus in his tribunate suggests that it was a somewhat later development—perhaps arising out of (and certainly given impetus by) the acquittal of M' Aquillius, the conqueror of Asia.[36] But once the new class had been created, it was an obvious development to assign it an important function; and this could not, under Roman conditions, be a function in actual government: C. Gracchus, as a second-century noble, had no conception of a state ruled by any body other than the Senate.[37] The myth that C. Gracchus wanted to raise a large number of *equites* to the Senate, based on a misunderstanding by our most miserable source and contradicted by everything else we know, has occasionally been revived.[38] It should be clear that it would make political nonsense. That scheme, when it did arise, came from a totally different motive and point of view: from M. Livius Drusus and L. Sulla, hoping to emasculate the (by then) politically conscious equestrian class by converting its most ambitious members into harmless backbenchers in the Senate.[39] The aims of C. Gracchus and his circle were the very opposite.

The year 129 is a crucial year, not only because of Scipio's death. It is worth rescuing from the obscurity due to the state of our sources and restoring to the importance that Cicero assigned to it. As it happens, a document of that same year shows the Senate still in action as the body supervising the *publicani* and, where necessary, protecting the provincials against them. In a decree of which two fragmentary copies have been found and which has been many times discussed,[40] we find both the consuls of 129, with a large advisory board (perhaps all senators, certainly all of senatorial families), hearing a dispute that had arisen between the *publicani* and the city of Pergamum over some boundaries. (The details are not easy to disengage from what we have.) King Attalus of Pergamum had bequeathed his kingdom to the Roman People in 133, and Tiberius Gracchus had seen to it that the bequest was accepted and had planned to use some of the royal funds in his agrarian schemes. Since then, there had been constant warfare in Asia, and the consul M' Aquillius must have been just about to leave for the war.[41] It is interesting to see the *publicani* happily settled in pursuit of their trade, no doubt on the royal land which was now public land of the Roman People.[42] The case was a major one: this is clear from the size and eminence of the advisory board, as well as from the presidency of both the consuls. In fact, the document is unique among surviving records of adjudications. The decision went against the *publicani*: this is clear from the fact that the city had the proceedings expensively recorded on stone. Presumably the income of the new public land had been sold by the censors of 131, and the dispute had arisen as the *publicani* first tried to collect. Although no money of the Roman State was immediately at stake,[43] the case must have concerned a considerable amount of money, to be heard in this fashion. Coming as it did in a year of violence and political agitation—the year of Scipio's action against the commission and his death; the year (as we have tried to show) of the separation of the new equestrian order from the Senate—it cannot be dissociated from the politics of the day; although, oddly enough, it is usually discussed from the antiquarian point of view, in isolation.

Forty years earlier, in 169, we could for the first time observe the influence of the *publicani* on the political actions of the officer class (still undivided). The adverse decision of 129, in a case of unique magnitude (as far as we know), must have made the *publicani* all the more ready to swallow (late in the same year) the 'bribe' of the constitution of a separate equestrian class, which they could hope to influence much more easily than the undivided officer class overawed by the presence of senators. Moreover: it was necessary for the commission to throw a 'bribe' to the *publicani*, if it was to hope for their support, since the Gracchan agrarian schemes worked against their interests. Not only in that, as land-owners, some of them (and especially the most important) were likely to be affected by the enforcement of the limit; but the permitted holdings (of 300 acres, plus perhaps additional land for children)[44] would now apparently be rent-free. This loss must not be exaggerated: as we have seen, it had proved difficult to collect from powerful holders of large areas. But such as it was, and added to any personal loss of land that some of them might be subject to, this aspect of the Gracchan law was likely to turn the *publicani* against the law rather than in its favour. Hence the 'bribe' was a political necessity, just as the 'bribe' to the Italians was soon seen to be. The issue of the case on the Asian land made the 'bribe' all the more effective, and acceptable.

It is not the mere chance of survival that shows us, precisely at this time, the first dispute (and at once the most important) over provincial tax revenues in which a Senate commission had to adjudicate.[45] The importance of these *uectigalia* was probably a recent development. There had always been taxes of some sort, in Rome as everywhere else. But the main tax had been the small property levy called *tributum*, directly collected, it seems (though we cannot be sure how).[46] Taxes on public land, and tolls and customs dues (*portoria*), were limited in extent and importance. The *publicanus* as customs officer appears in the plays of Plautus, early in the second century, as a standing joke: opening seals and nosing through the letters of people arriving from abroad.[47] Though this was no doubt taken over from Athenian originals, it must have been understood and enjoyed in Rome. A wife closely questioning her husband is told by him, in an outburst, that he seems to be married to a customs officer![48] But it was only in 199 that our sources first mention the censors as letting contracts for *portoria* at Capua and Puteoli,[49] old cities now subject to Rome: Capua had long been a commercial centre, while Puteoli was becoming the main port for Rome, and a colony was established there a few years later.[50] In 179, Livy tells us, a pair of very active censors (who spent a lot of money on building and, as we saw, had a year's public income allocated for it by the Senate) instituted many new *portoria* and other revenues.[51] After this, we have no actual record of new ones until the legislation of C. Gracchus, who was specially interested in public revenues.[52] In part this will be due to the loss of Livy's account after 167, the disastrous effects of which we have seen so many times; but in part perhaps simply to the fact that there were no major new developments—merely extensions of what had already been begun. By the end of the Republic,[53] we know that customs stations were collecting dues on behalf of companies of *publicani* in many (probably in all) major Italian and provincial cities and especially in the major seaports.

All this must have essentially developed in the second century, starting with the institution of the stations at Capua and Puteoli in 199, and greatly extended (perhaps already into the outlines of a scheme covering all of Roman Italy) by the censors of 179, whose activity is stressed. In Sicily—the oldest province—we see from the *Verrines* that *portoria* were (at least originally) sold separately for each city or small group of cities. In the rich eastern provinces, annexed much later, we find the *portoria* for the whole province sold together. It has been suggested[54] that this will mark the development from dues instituted one or two at a time to dues prescribed for a whole province (probably on annexation) and sold as a single lot. More probably, the law of Hiero (adapted to become the basic law of Roman Sicily) had established and maintained the Sicilian system, as it did in the case of the principal tax; except that the collection had in due course been transferred to Roman *publicani* and sold at Rome,[55] without being changed in its principles. In any case, by the middle of the second century only Sicily, Sardinia, and the two Spains were provinces; and only Sicily can have been profitable as regards *portoria*, however collected. Polybius gives us the evidence. In his account of the public contract business[56] he puts Italian building contracts ('too numerous to count') far at the head of the list, followed by various kinds of revenues. The implication is that the *ultro tributa* are still the most profitable part of the business; though, of course, we must remember that they gave rise to employment and general prosperity, as he also notes, and that this may be why he gives them preference.

The most interesting fact to notice is the transformation of the Roman tax and revenue system through the second century. As soon as possible after the Hannibalic War, the excess of *tributum* over the normal rate, which had had to be imposed during the War, was repaid out of booty. Then, in 167, after the triumph of L. Aemilius Paullus, the *tributum* was abolished. It is often said that henceforth Roman citizens paid no more taxes and lived on the proceeds of the empire. We have seen that this is quite untrue. The tax on the manumission of slaves continued, and *portoria* were gradually extended. We may speak of a change-over from reliance on a mixed system of direct and indirect taxation (with direct much the more important) to a system of wholly indirect taxation; and this also meant a change from a system relying largely on direct collection by the state to one relying wholly on *publicani*. It is not difficult to think of reasons for this. Above all, direct taxes are always more visible and more resented. But we may add that quite possibly the Treasury simply found, as indirect taxation was extended (especially by the reforms of 179), that it was much more efficiently collected.[57] This is suggested by the reforms of C. Gracchus, which will soon occupy us. How much Roman citizens now paid in taxes, compared with what they had paid as *tributum*, we simply do not know. It may be—but cannot be regarded as certain—that the large and increasing income from overseas relieved them of some burdens; but it may also be that the correspondingly increased commitments swallowed up much of the increase.

When the land of King Attalus became Roman in 133, *publicani* were sent out—no doubt after the next census (131/0)—to collect its revenues. The province of Asia, however, was organized only in 126, after a long war, and the settlement was ratified only in 125 or 124. We have no direct knowledge of the principles of organization.[58] But very soon after (in 123 or 122), C. Gracchus changed them. He introduced the revolutionary step of having the main tax of the whole of Asia (calculated as a tithe on agricultural produce) collected by Roman *publicani*, who hitherto had collected only minor taxes in the province. This meant that contracts would be sold by the censors, for five years at a time, for the richest province in Rome's possession.[59]

The sum was huge—quite unprecedented. Of course, the *publicani*, as we have seen, were ready for it, their organization vastly expanded over the preceding generation. Building contracts of (to our knowledge) up to 45 million denarii had recently been undertaken; the scope of revenue collection had been increasing for half a century; and we have seen the kind of sums that passed through their hands in the exploitation of the Spanish mines. But the evidence is clear that the profits of Asia, as a regular item, were overwhelming. In Cicero's day, before Pompey's conquests, the regular public revenues were said (by Pompey himself, who perhaps had an interest in depreciating them) to be 50 million denarii. At that time, Cicero stressed the fact that Asia provided a large part of the sum. Sixty years earlier, with about half the number of provinces and *portoria* not yet fully developed, the relative importance of Asia must have been much greater.[60] Though we cannot guess at figures, the effect must have been shattering when—probably in 123—this revenue first came in. That C. Gracchus was much concerned with revenue, we know from his own statement. I have tried to explain elsewhere[61] how he established the principle that the provinces of the Roman People were to be exploited for the benefit of the Roman People. Senatorial magistrates had shown themselves untrustworthy: several of them—most recently Aquillius, organizer of the province of Asia—were occupying their seats of honour in the Senate while it was widely believed that they were guilty of major peculation. C. Gracchus saw to it that this new goldmine of a province was not to be chiefly used to line the pockets of its governors and their staffs, whose corruption he attacked in his speeches.[62] The answer was obvious: to transfer the collection to the proved efficiency of the *publicani*. We have noted that, as far as taxes paid by Roman citizens were concerned, the Treasury had long ago decided to pursue the same course. Of course, they might be equally untrustworthy, a critic might object. But to this too the answer was obvious: it was the Senate's duty to supervise them; and as recently as 129 it had shown itself well capable of doing so. C. Gracchus, eminent Roman noble as he was, was merely restoring the balance of the state to what it ought always to have been: it was the duty of Senate and magistrates to govern and it was the proper sphere of the *publicani* to run public financial business. This would produce a healthy state of affairs, ultimately to the benefit of the Roman People and of the provincials themselves.[63]

But there was more than that wrong with the State, as had been shown by the fate of Tiberius Gracchus. The Senate had become over-powerful and had shown itself incapable of wisely using that power. Excessive power had corrupted it as an organ of government, and men like Gaius' brother had paid the penalty.[64] As early as 129, we found evidence that men had been thinking about this problem, and preparing remedies. The upper class had been split, so that the *equites* might be used to counterbalance the power of the Senate. If senators were to supervise the business contracts of the *publicani* as part of the normal activity of government, the new *equites* should be used to ensure that senatorial solidarity no longer led to the acquittal of senatorial malefactors. Hence the establishment of a court for cases of provincial extortion, a court shared by Senate and *equites,* to replace the senatorial one that had been in existence since 149 B.C. This (it seems) Gaius now claimed had been his brother Tiberius' idea; and this seems to be what he himself first proposed. In the end he was to go further: his law in its final form removed senators and their immediate relatives entirely from the court.[65]

The law that achieved this unfortunately survives in very imperfect form;[66] the positive qualifications of the jurors were twice mentioned, and chance has robbed us of them on both occasions. All we know is that magistrates, ex-magistrates, senators, and their immediate relatives (i.e. roughly the senatorial class) are excluded. Debate continues on whether the new jurors were defined by possession of the public horse, or by a financial qualification (of 100,000 denarii in property) which was the economic prerequisite for eligibility for equestrian status. Recently definition by strict equestrian status has been favoured.[67] The answer can never be certain. But it seems to me more likely that the wider category should be preferred. A well-known passage in Pliny,[68] as well as later history, seems to require it. I think C. Gracchus came to recognize that the officer class that had been separated from the Senate did not in itself provide a sufficient diversity of interest from the Senate itself, a sufficiently broad base on which to erect his edifice of the new balanced constitution. He therefore ended by ignoring the criterion of the public horse, defining his jurors by the purely financial criterion and thus creating a new class in the state: the class of jurors, as Pliny calls it. It was the logical continuation of what had been begun in 129. The *equites* had been split off from the old officer class and separated from the Senate; now they were to be brought into close association with men of equal wealth outside their class and with fewer personal connections with the senatorial families. In the age of Cicero we certainly find that the term *'eques'* is freely applied to all those who have the qualification. Pliny tells us that this was a slow development, starting with the Gracchan law; and we have no reason to disbelieve him.[69] The association on the juries ended by creating an expanded equestrian class, more remote than before from the Senate, and by almost obliterating, within that class, the distinction between those whose wealth was respectable and those whose wealth was not.[70]

Gaius is said by Cicero to have remarked that he had thrown daggers into the forum:[71] obviously (if genuine) a rhetorical exaggeration. More moderately, but still with disapproval, the historian Varro condemned him as 'having made the State two-headed' and thus prepared the way for civil war.[72] That might seem a just comment later. The necessities of politics had certainly led him further than he had intended. For he was, after all, a Roman noble, and we have seen that he could conceive—*popularis* though he was in his methods, and genuinely interested in the welfare of the common citizen—of no other way of governing the Republic but through the Senate. But, reactionary and corrupt as that body had shown itself, it had to be checked by a counterweight, which C. Gracchus and his associates (probably M. Fulvius Flaccus was one of their leaders in this) found in the creation of a separate *ordo equester* with a class consciousness of its own—a measure achieved at a favourable opportunity, when the Senate, by faithfully performing its function of governing, happened to have antagonized the *publicani* by an adverse decision. Henceforth the *publicani* could hope to dominate that truncated class. But in the end, I believe, C. Gracchus had gone further still: he had ended by directly challenging the unquestioned dogma of the moral superiority of landed wealth and had begun the process of enlarging the new equestrian order by associating it with other men of equal wealth, presumably not (on the whole) of that landed respectability which made the old-style *eques* no less than the senator. It was this larger class that was now to sit in judgment over senators, and thus to share in power, though not in government.

IV

The Public Companies

We have now reached the arrival of the *publicani* on the scene of major Roman politics with the legislation of C. Gracchus. Henceforth the danger is that an attempt to follow their history might expand into a history of the later Roman Republic. We must avoid this, even at the risk of taking much of the general historical background for granted. Inevitably, with evidence much more abundant and the *publicani* never far from the centre of the stage, we shall no longer need (or be able) to set out and discuss the whole of the available evidence: we shall be able to choose and to concentrate on what (I hope) is important and characteristic.

But before we proceed to follow the general history of the *publicani*, it will be useful to stop and consider how the large companies that will be the main subject of our investigation were in fact run. Fortunately, we now have enough evidence to give us a vivid picture; though inevitably many details are lacking, particularly as regards day-to-day activities. Still: how, without managerial training and schools of business administration, could the Romans organize companies that could handle contracts of a size dwarfing most private fortunes? Large figures, ancient or modern, tend to be meaningless; but let us recall that a building contract for 45 million denarii[1] was 450 times as much as the minimum property required for equestrian status. M. Crassus, reputed (perhaps wrongly) to be the richest man in Rome in the age of Caesar and Cicero, had a fortune that can be pretty accurately estimated at 8,000 talents,[2] i.e. 48 million denarii. The contract for building the Marcian adqueduct, as early as the middle of the second century, was of about the same value as the total fortune of the man who claimed to be Rome's leading millionaire a century later!

It is often said that the custom of forming associations rather than submitting individual bids is due to the increasing size of the sums involved, which individuals could not provide.[3] In fact, the custom was clearly an old one, and encouraged by the State—well established long before it became financially necessary to cope with the size of the contracts. As early as we can trace individual *publicani*—the three companies in the emergency of the Hannibalic War[4]—we find them already acting in association. As we saw, the average individual participation on that occasion was only in the range of 40,000 to 100,000 denarii—a large enough sum, to be sure, in its day, but small in comparison with figures we have since become accustomed to. Still, it might be said that it fully justified association. Our best example of the fact that association was practised without regard to the size of the sum is the only example we have of an actual contract agreement from the time of the Republic: not from Rome, as it happens, but from a Roman colony, where we may take it Roman law and custom was closely followed. In the year 105 B.C. the town council of Puteoli let a contract for the building of a wall in front of the temple of Serapis.[5] The specifications are carefully set out, and the total sum comes to 1,500 sesterces (375 denarii).[6] On this small contract, no fewer than five contractors sign. The chief of them is the bidder, who provides surety (acts as *praes*) in the amount mentioned. We know the Latin term for him—not mentioned in this inscription—was *manceps*.[7] This man normally had to offer some landed property to the Treasury as security for his ability to perform.[8] The status of the other four is not defined. But, to judge from what we know of Roman companies, they were probably the *socii*—the partners who made up the company. Here, as we have seen, they are not recorded as pledging any property; though it is possible that an equal sum is understood for each of them, or perhaps a quarter of the total sum each. Quite possibly, however, they have no obligation to the municipal treasury, which merely has to record their names. If so, it is the *manceps* alone whose property (as pledged) will be seized in case of non-fulfilment.

In bigger deals, more than one *praes* would be required: obviously, a contract running into millions would need more security than one man could or would offer. It has been thought, from the passage of Polybius in which he discusses the contracts, that secondary guarantors would be needed.[9] But it will be seen from the little contract at Puteoli that—whatever precisely the functions of the men listed—an association of a kind was formed as a matter of course even for a small contract. The obvious reason—though we cannot document it—is that the same company would bid for many contracts, some large and some small, and the same men (not always in association with one another) take part in even more. It therefore became advantageous (even where not actually necessary) to spread the risk,[10] both as regards *praedia* and as regards capital. The *praedes* would undoubtedly be *socii;* but if the Puteoli law is to be taken at face value, not all *socii* had to be *praedes*: you could apparently register as a contributor of capital and member of the association without having to pledge your own property.

The *socii*, in any case, had to be registered and constituted the company. They were the major contributors of capital; though we have no details on proportions or legal minima. Normally, Roman law did not know the concept of an association of individuals having a legal personality (*corpus*). But this could be specially conferred, and apparently was thus conferred on at least some companies of Roman *publicani*, so that they could, as companies, own property and transact business, just like any modern company.[11] With the large establishments known even for the second century—e.g. the 40,000 workers producing 9 million denarii of output in a single mining area in Spain[12]—this was obviously essential, from the State's point of view as from the contractors'. As we have seen, there is good reason to conclude that these establishments were not built up by one contracting firm, but—on the whole—were taken over when a new firm took over the contract concerned. We are not told in our source whether (and how) this right of legal personality was conferred on the companies under the Republic. But we have seen that it is almost necessary to assume it; and fortunately Tacitus provides the evidence: in a passage that has puzzled some commentators he tells us that in the days of the Republic these companies were established by consuls and tribunes.[13] It is therefore probable that at least the large companies (Tacitus says 'plerasque', which should imply that not all companies had this right), after purchasing a contract, were given certain privileges (including what added up to legal *corpus*) by a special law of the assembly. Unfortunately we do not know how far this extended. For instance, we do not know whether, with the death of a *manceps,* the company legally ceased to exist.[14] This would have led to untold complications in the case of large companies holding tax contracts for whole provinces, and one would think that part of the purpose of such a grant, from the State's point of view, was to ensure the continuity of the company for the duration of the contract. But these and other legal puzzles cannot be firmly resolved on our evidence.

Apart from the *socii,* Livy once mentions another class of members, the *adfines*:[15] in the troubles of 169 they, along with *socii,* are excluded from the new censorial contracts. We simply have no idea who they are. If there were personal secondary guarantors,[16] of lesser status than full *socii,* the word may apply to them. But as we have seen, there is no reason to think that even all the *socii* necessarily had to pledge property. Nor, on the other hand, are the *adfines* mere anonymous shareholders (as we shall see): it is clear that they, like the *socii,* were on the censors' register, and that they had (at least in theory) some responsibility for the running of the company. (Else there would have been no reason for excluding them when things had gone wrong.) The answer is probably, as so often, to be sought in the fact that our literary sources do not use such terms in precise technical meanings. Cicero, for instance, never mentions the *adfines;* and it may well be that they were merely a (less privileged) class of *socii*—the term that, in Cicero, covers all members.

The contract was made between the *manceps* and the presiding magistrate (normally a censor for regular contracts—but as we have already seen, it could be a praetor or (no doubt) a consul). It was the magistrate who set out the conditions of the contract, no doubt before the bidding. As we have seen, he had—as Roman magistrates normally had—a great deal of latitude in formulating them: conditions for admission to, or exclusion from, the auction could be arbitrarily specified. But, as again was usual in Rome, the contract for a particular purpose (the *lex censoria*) gradually assumed 'tralatician' form; i.e., it was handed on in much the same way from one magistrate to the next, with only occasional additions in the light of experience (or, perhaps, special circumstances). So much was this so that particular new clauses, in standard contracts, were known by the names of the censors who had introduced them.[17] Certain features seem to have been standard for all *leges*. The Puteoli contract probably gives us a good idea of some of them. There was a *dies operis* (completion date) and a *dies pecuniae* (date of payment) in all contracts for goods and services; and there was a clause providing for *probatio*: official inspection and approval of the work by the magistrate who had sold the contract or his successor, or by a specially appointed committee.[18] At Puteoli—and again, we may be sure that this was copied from Roman practice—half the sum was paid when the *praedia* were duly assigned, the other half after completion and inspection. We know from the actions of Verres (if we subtract the element of personal chicanery!) that the process of inspection was something that the contractor had to take very seriously: he seems to have been completely at the mercy of the inspecting magistrate, apparently without right of appeal.[19] It would be still more interesting if we had a similar specimen of a contract for revenue collection. But we do not. We cannot tell to what extent it was parallel. The chances are—given the Roman love of precedent—that on the whole it was: at least to the extent that the contractor had to pay a large sum in advance, and the rest either in instalments or at the end of the *lustrum*. This would help to explain the particularly large size of the *societates* that bought the provincial taxes.

We also know that the standard contract included—at least for tax collection; but again, probably also for *ultro tributa*, where there would be as good reason for it—a clause indemnifying the contractor in case of enemy action.[20] Whether also against natural disaster, we are not told in any surviving source; and on the whole it is perhaps unlikely that we should not have heard of it. We must also remember that insurance for supplies carried by sea had been added as a special concession in the Hannibalic War— and the result had not been such as to encourage continuation.[21] In any case, however, the insurance against enemy action greatly lessened the risk: the Roman government apparently recognized that it had the responsibility of providing safe conditions within the sphere it controlled. (Natural disaster, of course, could not be prevented by the State, and any State action to relieve those affected was always *ex gratia*, and is rarely heard of in the Republic.)

However, we must in any case not think of *publicani*—as their modern critics tend to do[22]—as merely shovelling in the money. A major war—as Cicero makes clear in the speech on behalf of

Manilius' law—destroyed far more than could be made good by mere remission of the contract price: we have seen that vast capital investments were needed. And natural disaster (if not covered by the State—as we have seen, there is no sign that it was) must also have been a considerable risk, in ancient conditions. Complaints can be exaggerated, as when Cicero wants to arouse resentment against a personal enemy who, as governor, kept the *publicani* on a tight rein; and we shall see that he himself thought the most famous application for relief—that of the Asian *publicani* in 61—a piece of mere impudence. But we do, at least in one case, have an actual name of a young friend of Cicero's—M. Terentius Varro Gibba—who lost money as a *publicanus* and had to practise as a barrister for some time in order to recoup his losses and be able to enter upon an official career.[23] And the civil wars at the end of the Republic were, of course, quite disastrous for many of them.[24]

As we have seen, the *socii* (whatever precisely the *adfines* were) constituted the company. Letters from their provincial agents were addressed to the *socii*, and Cicero frequently mentions such correspondence. The *socii* of large companies met from time to time for formal purposes, rather like modern shareholders, and (it seems) with no more real power. We find the whole multitude of *socii* assembled to honour the returning governor C. Verres, as was customary on such occasions.[25] They are then dismissed, while an important decision is taken on their behalf by other people. It all sounds familiar. The executive power was in the hands of officials called *magistri*. Presumably one of them might be the *manceps;* but we have no precise information. The number of *magistri* no doubt varied according to the size of the company and the complexities of its business. In the one case where Cicero gives us details—a relatively small company active in Sicily—the board of directors consists of three men, apparently of unequal *auctoritas*: P. Vettius Chilo, a distinguished *eques Romanus*, seems very much the man in charge. The other two (P. Servilius and C. Antistius) are *scribae*:[26] men usually of undistinguished origin, although the perquisites of office enabled them quite often (it seems) to rise high, even to equestrian status.[27] It is amusing to note the difference in the words of praise applied to these three men: P. Vettius Chilo, a Roman knight related to at least one senator (Verres' own quaestor), is *honestissimus atque ornatissimus* (the latter an epithet reserved for members of the upper class); the two *scribae* are *primi homines atque honestissimi*. In any case, these men write official letters on behalf of the company, and Vettius is the one who actually composes them. It seems that these directors changed annually; or at least some of them did. For when Cicero wanted to know to whom to go for records of the time of Verres' Sicilian governorship (73 - 71 B.C.), he found out who had been the *magistri* in charge of company records during those years; and he found that in the year that concerned him the *magister* in charge of records had been one L. Vibius, also a Roman knight.[28] In the year of the trial (70) the post was held by a L. Tullius—despite his name a friend of Verres' and apparently not of Cicero's—in whose house Cicero also searched for documents.[29] The evidence conclusively suggests annual election, at least to this post; and it also shows us that there was a certain amount of specialization among the *magistri*. In an interesting sidelight, we learn[30] that the *magister* in charge of records usually kept copies of all documents for himself when he handed the file over to his successor—no doubt often greatly to his personal profit. No one tells us how *magistri* were elected. It may have been (in principle, at any rate—in practice there would no doubt be an oligarchy similar to that of a modern company) by simple election on the part of the *socii*.

This brings us to a mysterious body, only once mentioned in all our literature,[31] the *decumani*. When Verres returned from Sicily, as we have seen, the *socii* of the company concerned met him in a body to express their ritual thanks. After this, however, there was serious business to be discussed: relations between Verres and the company had originally been very bad, since he had from the start tried to cheat them over export duty. It was only after firm reaction from the *magistri* that he apparently thought better of it and let them have a share of his spoils in compensation. This is why the company was, in the end, officially satisfied with his administration: it had lost less than it had gained. However, there remained incriminating (and, in the circumstances, embarrassing) letters in the files, written during the period of initial discord. After Verres' return, on his strong urging, these were dealt with. When the *socii* had duly welcomed him, they were dismissed and a friend of Verres (unnamed) who happened to be a *magister* summoned a meeting of the *decumani*, who decreed that the incriminatory letters should be destroyed, so as not to provide possible evidence against Verres. (It was copies of these letters that Cicero went to search for, as we saw, at the private residence of an ex-*magister*.) Now, who are the *decumani*?

The word can mean simply 'farmers of the tithe'; but this is not the meaning here, since the company concerned was not a tithe-farming one; moreover, the *decumani* (in the tithe-farming sense) in Sicily were rather humble folk.[32] These men, however, were important: it is they who take an extremely dubious decision in secret, in the absence of the majority of the *socii*—but apparently carried out by the company.[33] Carcopino long ago suggested that they were the governing body of the company. Since then, an inscription has attested the use of 'decumanus' in the technical sense of 'head of a section' (*decuria*) of an organization.[34] Nicolet has argued from this that the company concerned (and probably others) was divided into such *decuriae,* each headed by an important man. These could no doubt be used as voting units in the election of *magistri,* to ensure the election of the right men. The explanation is persuasive, and may well be correct. But an alternative should be considered. Cicero's references to the men concerned are perhaps extravagant, inappropriate (even if we bear the needs of his case in mind) for the governing body of what was after all rather a minor company (as we shall soon see). Not only are they all Roman knights, as appears from the passage concerned; but he goes so far as to call them 'the leaders and, as it were, the senators of the *publicani*' (note that he does not say 'of a company'); and some of them, present in court and willing to testify, are 'leaders of the equestrian order', and 'most honourable and most wealthy men'.[35]

Were these men, as Cicero's language *prima facie* implies, the governing body of the whole *ordo* of *publicani*? No such body is attested, even though the word 'ordo' is freely used of the *publicani*; and it may imply—as it always seems to, when in serious and technical use—some kind of organization.[36] Such a body may have acted as a political pressure group, such as we know the *publicani* in fact were in the late Republic.[37] We shall see that, in Cicero's day (though a little after the date of the *Verrines*), the ties among all the companies were particularly close, so as to constitute a cartel. The organization then revealed probably goes back, at least in some form, for some years. In fact, what may have happened on this occasion may be interpreted as the *magister*'s successful attempt to assure himself of the support of the whole *ordo* for an action of very dubious legality. There might obviously—although Cicero, for personal reasons, chooses not to make an issue of it—be much to be said about this action of destroying some of the company's documents that might be of public interest. The accounts (*tabulae*) of a company were public documents. Court orders could secure access to them, as indeed to the company's records.[38] But the *tabulae* were so carefully protected by law that even a court order could not secure their removal to Rome: all that Cicero could do was to have notarized copies made.[39] In the circumstances, one might conjecture what a hostile prosecutor might have made of the fact that letters throwing necessary light on those *tabulae* had been secretly destroyed. Hence, perhaps, the need for more than a decision by the *magistri* (who, surely, would otherwise have been technically competent to handle such matters): a cautious attempt to make sure in advance of the support of the *ordo* as a whole, which might deter any prosecutor from pressing the matter. In this, at any rate, they succeeded.[40]

In the provinces the *socii* (i.e. the company) were represented by officers called *pro magistro*.[41] How many of these there were, in each province, and how free they were to act on their own initiative, we cannot tell. This probably varied greatly according to the circumstances: the size and nature of the province and of the company itself. In spite of their official title, these men were not elected by the *socii* in Rome, but were paid employees of the company, therefore probably appointed by the directors. The phrase used of them ('operas dare')[42] implies, in the Roman aristocratic view of things, a rather lowly station in life. And so it had no doubt started out, from the point of view of Rome, however powerful the person concerned might appear to those whose money he collected. The *pro magistro* was in charge of the keeping of the accounts as well as of collecting the actual taxes; but we see from the *Verrines* that he was expected to send official reports to the *magistri* in Rome and, in particular, inform them of anything beyond his ability to remedy—such as an attempt by a governor (with all a governor's power and *auctoritas*) to avoid paying taxes; but also of his relations with the governor in general: it is clear that the favourable report of their *pro magistro* is what in the end brings about the decision of the company to express its official gratitude to Verres. We know very few of these men by name and can say little about their station in life, except (again) that it must have varied enormously according to the business done.

In Sicily, while Verres was governor, the same company had bought both the pasture-tax (*scriptura*) and the *portorium* (at least of Syracuse).[43] Its representatives in Sicily are two men with quite undistinguished names, L. Canuleius and L. Carpinatius, the former in charge of the *portorium*, the latter in charge of the *scriptura*.[44] Carpinatius turned out to be one of Verres' chief collaborators and fellow-profiteers, to some extent to the advantage of his company. When Cicero first introduces this man, he refers to him as 'quidam L. Carpinatius'. The epithet is decisive and socially damning: this was not a man whom Roman senators were expected to know.[45] This cannot be done to eminent men, even if they are friends of Verres.

We may contrast the name of the only other certainly known *pro magistro*, P. Terentius Hispo. This man, a friend of Cicero's, is warmly recommended to the governor of Bithynia in 51, after Cicero himself (he admits) has vainly tried to intervene on his behalf with the city of Ephesus.[46] Hispo was at that time in charge of the *scriptura* of Bithynia: a strange state of affairs that will have to occupy us again. By 47, Hispo has apparently retired, though he is still living in Asia. It was at that time that he met the Quinti Cicerones, Cicero's brother and nephew, and informed Cicero of their unexpected hostility towards him (Cicero); apparently Hispo did his best (unsuccessfully) to change their minds.[47] Cicero here describes him as the man 'who was *pro magistro* in Asia for *scriptura* and *portoria*'. Both these important contracts—for the whole of Asia, it seems—had therefore been in the hands of the same company. (We recall that even thirty years earlier the grazing-tax and at least one (probably six) of the customs points in Sicily had been managed by the same company.) Since we are still in the same quinquennium, it seems to follow that the *scriptura* for both Bithynia and Asia, as well as the customs dues for Asia, had been in the hands of the same company at the same time, and all managed by Hispo. (We recall his dealings with Ephesus in 51.) We may, in the circumstances, fairly confidently add the customs dues of Bithynia—not mentioned by Cicero in 51 simply because it was not to the point of his immediate recommendation. Hispo, no doubt, was in charge of tens of thousands of employees, over his vast area of responsibility. It is not surprising to find the citizens of one of the cities setting up a statue in honour of his wife—who is a daughter of a Q. Sulpicius, of distinguished family and quite possibly related to a consul.[48] This great man is far removed from 'a certain Carpinatius' in Sicily, in (technically) the same position.[49]

By Cicero's day, the companies performed important services for the State, quite apart from the principal service of the public (and especially tax) contracts. Thus they had the only efficient postal service (the State had none at all), and we find their couriers (*tabellarii*) taking letters to and from provincial governors as a matter of course.[50] They could also act as State bankers: again the State itself had nothing of the sort. Since the Romans had no banknotes, the only way of avoiding the awkward and risky transfer of large sums of cash to and from every province every year was by a system of bank drafts. But the sums involved were so large, by private standards of business, that no private *negotiator* would have been able to deal with them. Moreover, it was, of course, the *publicani* who had physical possession of the actual cash they collected. It thus became possible for the Senate to authorize drafts on the provincial office of a company when it allocated a sum for supplies to a governor. (This was called *ornare prouinciam*.) The company concerned would keep the revenues it had collected until the governor came to claim his grant. We have no evidence for this practice before Sulla; though one might expect it to develop naturally out of the Gracchan system, which gave the *publicani* the major part of Roman revenues to handle. In any case, as early as the seventies, Verres received a grant for the purchase of wheat in the form of a draft on the local office of the company we have already had to discuss in some detail: the company that held the pasture tax and some of the customs dues in Sicily and that must—although small by Asian standards— have been the largest company active in Sicily.[51] The money thus allocated was not, of course, expected to be all drawn at once; and the company was (in strict law) under an obligation to pay the State interest for the time that the money remained in its charge. But it appears that the Senate, as a matter of grace, sometimes (or usually?) allowed the company to keep the interest, which might be quite properly regarded as a banker's charge for the important service rendered.[52] Verres, of course, found a way more profitable to himself: he drew the money at once and invested it with the company itself at 24 per cent interest in his own name—at which the senior *magister* of the company grew furious, threatening to make Verres repay the interest to the company on his return to Rome, unless he could prove he had paid it over to the State (which he had no intention of doing).[53]

Similarly, the outgoing governor might leave any surplus he had at the end of his administration—this seems to have been rather a rare event, since his staff and suite expected the profits to be distributed to them[54]—with the local *publicani* and get a receipt and surety for it. The honest Cicero thus deposited 1 million sesterces,[55] after taking a perfectly legal personal profit of 2,200,000 for himself.[56] Probably not all *societates* were capable of handling the large sums that might be involved, particularly in the grant for a province. A great deal must have depended on whether the province was, on the whole, profitable, or whether it had to be subsidized by the exchequer. If the latter, there would obviously not be enough money in the province for the governor's supply grant. In any case, we may note that L. Piso, Caesar's father-in-law, as eager as Verres to profit from the money officially allocated to him, made a different arrangement: he drew the whole of his grant in Rome in 58 and then invested it from there in his own name.[57] It should be added, however, that he was on bad terms with the *publicani*.

It must always be borne in mind that companies must have varied enormously in the size and profitability of the undertakings. The difference between P. Terentius Hispo and L. Carpinatius is that between a really front-rank and a middle-grade company (the latter still quite respectable in its day). We hear nothing whatever about (say) the companies that farmed the *portoria* in Sardinia or the *scriptura* in Macedonia. Most of our detailed evidence comes from the *Verrines,* practically all the rest concerns the lucrative provinces of the East. As a result, our picture is inevitably a little distorted—as though we tried to recreate the working of a modern Western economy from evidence limited to some of the large international corporations. We have seen that *publicani* could lose their fortunes. That is less surprising than it seems to those who do not bear all the conditions in mind. The minor *uectigalia* of the earlier provinces (i.e. the less lucrative ones, by comparison with the East) were in the hands of the *publicani,* and we have seen that large enough sums were involved, even if small by comparison with five years' Asian tithe. But these investments must have been highly speculative. In the absence of statistics on trade and production, and with great variations in prices attested, no one could be sure how much salt would be sold or what the customs dues of a province would be worth over the next five years. Some records (e.g. of contract prices) were obviously kept; but there must have been a great deal of variation, and some disappointment. The main tax (the agricultural tithe) of an Eastern province was more satisfactory: very accurate records had been kept even by the kings, the Romans' predecessors; and it was generally agreed that this tax, despite the risks from nature and enemies, was the most profitable one, for both Rome and the collectors. However, in the older provinces this basic tax was (as far as we know) never collected by Roman *publicani*. For a long time, Asia must have been the only province where this was done: there are no others we can be really sure of until Bithynia was left to the Roman People in 74, conquered by L. Lucullus and organized by Pompey.

The collectors, naturally, took what they could get away with. By the time of the *Verrines,* additional charges (going beyond the legal limit) had gradually become customary, and even honourable governors would connive at their being extorted. One of the main features of interest in the *Verrines* is, in fact, Cicero's admission of what has become normal and acceptable in provincial adminis-tration. Light is thrown on senators and their staffs; but this does not concern us here. We must in the main keep to *publicani*. In theory, the amount of the tithe was fixed at one tenth of the pro-duce: it would not only be in Sicily that the landowner could not legally be forced to pay more, so that it might seem to be in-different to him whether or not the company had overpaid for its contract;[58] and according to law, if the collector did not obtain what he regarded as the right amount, he had to proceed through the governor's court and ask for judgment in the amount claimed.[59] But we see Verres overturning this custom in Sicily, where it seemed (on account of the *lex Hieronica*) more firmly anchored than anywhere else; and although it is very likely that Verres' successor L. Metellus returned to the previous arrangement in this as in other respects,[60] it is clear that even the most elementary principles of protection and justice for the provincial depended on the whim (and probity) of the governor. It would take us too far to follow this through in detail. It is not often recognized how unsystematic and how dependent on the character and pur-poses of the individual the whole of provincial administration under the Republic really was: one tends to see it in terms of the system slowly developed under the Empire.

It was the governor who ultimately controlled the *pactiones*—the agreements that were the key operation in the whole routine of tax collection. In Sicily the *pactio* was between the *publicanus* and the individual farmer; in the East it was between him and the city, which then proceeded to have the amount agreed upon col-lected by its own (basically similar) methods. The *pactio* settled the amount that both sides recognized was due. Once this agree-ment had been reached, only minor points of fact (whether payment had been made, whether the grain was of adequate quality, or such matters) remained to be decided. It was the *pactio* that gave the governor his main chance if he was unscrupulous, his main worry if he was honest. Nothing gave Cicero—eager to acquire an untarnished reputation in Cilicia, without offending the *publicani* —more pleasure than to hear that the *pactiones* for his year had already been settled before his arrival.[61] That was written when he arrived at Ephesus. An experience that he does not mention at the time must have shown him how lucky he was: when (as we saw) he tried to intervene with the Ephesians—who were not in his province, but who had received him royally, as though he were their own governor[62]—on behalf of his friend P. Terentius Hispo, to persuade them to agree to a *pactio* on pasture tax as a favour to himself, he got nowhere.[63] The governor, of course, had stronger means of persuasion, as Cicero, in supporting his friends. politely points out to one or two.[64] Verres in Sicily makes it quite clear what a mixture of force and pseudo-legal chicanery was at his disposal if he chose to use it. As we saw, he arbitrarily and contrary to all precedent allowed the collector to collect what he regarded as proper and made the *farmer* sue for redress, in his (Verres') court—with so little hope of success that there was not a single such suit during his tenure.[65] By his methods he enabled his favourite tax collectors (who shared their profit with him) to arrive at *pactiones* that were—as Cicero proves in a long and heart-rending catalogue of precise detail—ruinous to the victims.

In his letter to his brother Quintus on the responsibilities of provincial government, Cicero gives him cautious advice on his most difficult assignment: how to preserve the provincials from ruin without offending the *publicani,* on whom the political future of both the brothers depends.[66] He begins by pointing out the benefits of peace and security that Rome is conferring on Asia, and for which her taxation is a just return. (This only three years after the end of the war with Mithridates, in which Asia was devastated.) He continues to argue that the Asian Greeks have shown themselves incapable of making payments without *publicani* (which is probably true: it was an old tradition in Greek cities and Hellenistic kingdoms) and therefore have no right to complain about the Roman ones. Finally, Quintus is to give them good advice: they can save themselves a lot of trouble if they do not insist on their rights under the *lex censoria;* and this will also give them the satisfaction of having assisted the two

Ciceros in maintaining their political alliance with the *publicani*.

The most serious point to save in this display of priggish complacency is the fact that it was by now obviously regarded as unusually foolish for a provincial to insist on the terms of the *lex censoria*—which, i.a., guaranteed him the right not to pay more than the legal ten per cent. This, as is clear, must have led to his being persecuted by the *publicani* (and they could only do this with the connivance of the governor) to such an extent that the saving was not worth while. Certainly, it was difficult to protect them without making powerful political enemies. This was by no means new. We see in the *Verrines* how the governor himself could add on certain extras that in fact went to his staff: such items as 'inspection fee' and 'exchange fee' and even 'sealing-wax fee' had become standard items under Verres; and Cicero implies that, although they were not yet universal, they were by no means unknown elsewhere.[67] Similarly he could admit and support illicit charges by the *publicani*, such as the 'collection fee' of one per cent or more, which seems to have become standard in Cicero's day and which must have greatly diminished the risk and added to the profit.[68] In what other respects the *lex censoria* was usually infringed, we simply do not know. But once the principle was established, it was clearly difficult to draw the line. It would more than ever depend on the character of the governor: we have already seen that it was not easy for him to be honest.

That the companies also engaged in moneylending in order to employ their vast cash resources is obvious. L. Carpinatius, in Sicily, had lent Verres' victims money so that they could pay for the governor's rapacity.[69] This must have been common practice in the Eastern provinces, where the cities were often hopelessly in debt and the *publicani* had most of the money. We shall see evidence for their large-scale activities in one or two famous instances. It has also been suggested that they went in for commerce;[70] but the evidence for this is poor, and it is clear that (as we might expect) their interests could be opposed to those of traders.[71]

These were the companies that, after the legislation of C. Gracchus, and particularly in the age of Cicero, played such an important part in Roman politics. We can now sketch the history of their influence.

V

Equites, Senators, Armies

We have tried to put together much of what can be gathered about the working and the organization of the big companies in the age of Cicero. Something has already emerged about their relations with the State (and with both the Senate as a body and individual senators). More will emerge in due course. For we must now—without (I repeat) yielding to the temptation of writing a history of the late Republic—try to give a brief picture of the place of the companies in that history.

There is very little evidence on the generation immediately following the death of C. Gracchus. As we saw, he tried to redress the balance of political power by calling in the wealthiest citizens not of senatorial rank to sit in judgment on senators: they were to have no executive or decision-making function: that was for the Senate, as always. But by their judicial prerogative they were both to prevent the selfish exploitation of provincials by magistrates and their senatorial friends and to make the Senate more responsible in governing. Moreover, the intention was clearly to provide jurors for all criminal trials not heard by the People. Whether C. Gracchus himself established other courts, we cannot tell; nor what he did about civil cases.[1] But the jury panels, elaborately selected by the praetor, were available; and (whether or not

there was a law to that effect) it seems that over the next generation they were used both for regular courts set up on the model
of the extortion court[2] and for special tribunals, such as those
that tried the Vestals and the political victims of the Mamilian
Commission: the two most famous special trials before 91 B.C.[3]
It was on these courts—if the view here presented is correct—that
the traditional *equites* met and gradually fused with those of equal
wealth outside the exclusive class of the recipients of the
'public horse', until (by the sixties, at the latest) they all claimed
the title of '*equites*'. The effect (almost certainly planned by C.
Gracchus and his friends) was to do away, within that class, with
the exclusive stress on landed property as the basis for social
eminence and political power. The traditional *equites*, as we saw,
were still brought up within that scheme of social values; even
though their peculiar association with the public companies had
given them new interests and must, in at least some cases, have
led to finance taking precedence over land as the basis of their
own wealth.[4] Those outside the order would no doubt still invest
in Italian land in order to acquire respectability; but their financial
base would be largely outside it, in the variety of activities (chiefly
financial) that the Romans called *negotia;* and many of them,
inevitably, would be led to take part in the most lucrative of
financial activities, the public companies, still largely led by
eminent *equites*.

It was in this way that the class later called the *equites*—and
much wider than those who had held the public horse—came
into being, over more than a generation. Pliny, in a crucial passage,
tells us that originally they were called the 'jury class':[5] this,
clearly, was what they had in common, whether holders of the
public horse or merely rich enough to be technically qualified for
this special distinction. The Gracchan juries—soon, as we saw,
expanded beyond the old extortion court, and with opportunities
for service on the panels for special investigations—completed the
work begun by the Gracchans, as a consequence of the state of
public affairs revealed by the failure and death of Tiberius
Gracchus: the holders of the public horse, separated from the
Senate, were moved closer to those outside the political class who
shared their basic interest in non-landed wealth. Hence, during the
generation that follows, inevitable confusion in our sources, as we
can never be quite sure whether those using the word '*equites*'
or its Greek equivalent are using it strictly or (by anticipation) in
its wider, Ciceronian, sense. Nor do we know when the process of

absorption was complete. It is now generally recognized that
the practical disappearance of the census after Sulla had much
to do with it. There was only one successful census between 86
B.C. and the time of Augustus: that was in 70 B.C., part of the
ostentatious 'restoration of the Republic' that marked the end of
the Sullan oligarchy in its political definition.[6] The censors, inevitably, compiled a new register of holders of the public horse.[7] As
the number of citizens, with the first proper registration of the
Italians, rose to 910,000, it is possible that they were correspondingly generous in assigning the public horse; though, as a recent
scholar found, it is annoyingly impossible to find out whether any
of the numerous characters attested as *equites* after this time in
fact possessed it.[8] Another step was to come: in 67, the tribune L.
Roscius Otho 'restored' to the *equites* their old privilege of special
seats at the games. It is to be conjectured that he defined the term
in the current 'popular' sense, by property.[9] The definition was disliked by the People, who were opposed to having a new privileged
element marked out. (The privileges of the traditional *equites* were
well established, even if this one had at some time been lost.) And
—more decisive still—Cicero praises the measure and describes it
as hailed by all, before a court that included one third *tribuni
aerarii*.[10] Now, whoever precisely those were, they were not holders
of the public horse; and if Cicero is so enthusiastic about the law
in front of that audience, in a case that he was obviously trying
to win, it follows that they benefited by the law or were at any
rate not among those infuriated by it. In fact, it has been plausibly
suggested that they may have been the men qualified by property
for equestrian rank, but not placed on the last censors' list of
equites.[11] This, if true, would clinch the argument.

We seem to have been led out of our way, in pursuit of that
nightmare or will-o'-the-wisp of modern scholarship, the *ordo
equester*. However, it is essential to have some ideas on that subject
if we are to discuss the *publicani,* so closely associated with it in
Cicero and in modern works.

Of course, the *equites* in the new sense of the word never became
a homogeneous class, any more than even the *equites* of the second
century had been.[12] A large number of them were still basically
land-owners, and we must imagine most of them happily engaging
in the social round and the local squabbles in their country town,
with little lasting interest in the electoral and political struggles
in Rome.[13] Nor did they pursue a single political line: all those
—from C. Gracchus through Saturninus and Glaucia to the *popu-*

lares of the late Republic—who relied on their support and political gratitude found out their inconsistency; as did, from another point of view, men like Cicero, trying to create harmony between Senate and *equites.* They did, however, come to form—as Gracchus had planned—a *tertium corpus* in the body politic (to use Pliny's famous phrase):[14] a 'middle class' between Senate and People, in the literal sense of the word—though not, as some have been misled into thinking, in the sense that this term has acquired in modern historical and sociological writing, implying anti-aristocratic interests and bias.

It is some time before we can trace any particular prominence on the part of the *publicani.* For a generation, what most arouses the ire of the new class is any attack on the privilege that gives it substance: its possession of the courts. Attempts were made to remove that privilege, and it is interesting that one of them (by the consul Q. Caepio, in 106) succeeded. at a time of temporary ascendancy for the traditional noble leaders, who appeared to have been justified by Marius' failure to redeem his promise of swift victory in Numidia.[15] Cicero later cites an attempt to praise Caepio's law in front of *equites* as an example of offence to the audience—an error the orator must at all costs avoid; and it is interesting to see that L. Crassus, supporting the bill, made his famous appeal to the People to 'snatch us [i.e. senators] out of the jaws of those whose cruelty cannot even be assuaged by our blood'. This was the *magistra oratio* that Cicero learnt by heart in his youth, not many years after it had been delivered.[16] The reference, presumably, must have had some superficial plausibility; it cannot be to the extortion court, which, at this time, shows, as far as our sources enable us to see, no sign of bloodthirsty political justice.[17] No, the reference is to the special courts, and particularly the Mamilian Commission, with its 'Gracchan jurors';[18] its harshness became proverbial, and it is clear that its main motive was political vendetta.[19] The events would be in everybody's minds, only three years later; and the speech underlines the main reason for the revulsion in feeling. The Numidian War and the supposed venality of the nobles had been the pretext for condemning several nobles; but now the Numidian War was under Marius' command, and going no better. The short snippet we have suggests part of the argument that must have (as it did) carried conviction. But on a longer view, Crassus thought he had found the answer to Gracchus' policy. The new class must be restrained by collaboration between Senate and People. The Senate was both the patron and, politically, the servant of the People—or so political theory in rhetorical form could allege. Given a chance, and some persuasion, the People would return to its allegiance and its trust in the *fides* of those who had always led it. The new class—unlike even the traditional *equites*—had no roots and could not expect any loyalty; nor did the broadening of the economic base appeal to the People as a whole: there was little advantage to most citizens in political power given to the rich, whom they mainly knew as tax-collectors and moneylenders. The programme was promising, and others were to take it up when the time seemed ripe and Crassus had passed on his ideas to a younger generation.[20] In terms of political calculation, this line seemed promising. Of the two Roman assemblies, the tribal assembly was perhaps more open to influence by local Italian aristocrats, who would all be (on the wider definition) *equites*—particularly so, of course, after the enfranchisement of the whole of Italy. That assembly was heavily weighted against city residents; and it must have been easy to bring in loyal supporters for a special occasion. In the centuriate assembly, where the votes were weighted in favour of wealth, the first class (which held most of the power) still had a property qualification only one tenth (or at most one quarter) that of the *equites*. Though wealthy by the standards of the impoverished majority, these men were small fry and did not necessarily share the equestrian outlook; though it may be assumed that they had shares in the public companies. It would be interesting to know which assembly Caepio used to pass his jury law: as consul he had access to both. But we have no evidence. Certainly, it was the tribal assembly (or, more probably, the Meeting of the Plebs, organized on similar lines) that before long restored the courts to the *equites*.[21]

We have had to dwell on the formation and foundations of that broader body of '*equites*' which, in the late Republic, is often the political base of the *publicani*. For some time, as we have already mentioned, there is no evidence for this. Trials of provincial governors—especially from Asia, where the companies had a much larger stake than anywhere else—ought to have reflected political power on the part of those companies. In fact, not one governor of Asia is known to have been convicted, and one was acquitted in a striking case.[22] Not that—as tended to be the case in the permissive and corrupt atmosphere of the late Republic—there were no convictions at all: several are recorded, including the famous one of a governor of Macedonia, at which the damages were assessed at a trivial sum.[23] No complaint appears in the sources, and there are acquittals as well.[24] The conclusion must be that, although in any one case there might be a miscarriage of justice (on the whole in the direction of leniency: we have evidence of what an orator could do),[25] the trials were as fair as could be expected and C. Gracchus' scheme was working well enough. If the *publicani* were using the courts as a means of political blackmail, they were singularly unsucessful at it. It is easier to believe that, on the whole, the idea had not occurred to them. Cicero, in a well-known passage, says that during all the time *equites* sat on the courts, there was never the slightest breath of suspicion that a juror had been corrupted.[26] However much we may allow for the orator's exaggeration, it is a tribute to the work and thought of C. Gracchus. And we may well add (what was not pertinent to Cicero's case and, for one well-known reason, could in any case not be said) that there is no suspicion of dispensing political justice.

It might be thought that governors were afraid to act against the interests of their future judges. Again, there is no evidence that the *publicani* inspired particular awe or were above the *imperium* and *auctoritas* of a Roman magistrate. Indeed, there is some to the contrary. The first inkling we have of misbehaviour by them is not in a province at all, but in a client state adjacent to one. In fact, the first complaint (and it was to turn out to be important beyond what could be suspected) came from Nicomedes III of Bithynia. When asked to contribute forces for the war against the Germans in 104, he replied that he had not enough manpower left: most of his subjects had been sold off into slavery by the *publicani*![27] This reply came as such a shock to the Senate that it at once decreed that no citizen of an allied (i.e. client) state should be held in slavery in a Roman province. It is clear that the Senate had not known what was going on; and that, knowing it, it acted promptly and vigorously. And it is clear that what had happened was in no way due to fear of the *publicani*. On the contrary, the complaint had not come from a Roman province. The *publicani* based in Asia had been adding to their gains by doing business outside the area under the control of a Roman governor. We can see, half a century later, that it might still be easier to get away with dubious means of making a profit in an allied kingdom than in a well-run province; and, in fact, that the governor who kept his province under strict control might not hesitate to be more permissive in his attitude to what went on outside. When Cicero was asked to give a troop of cavalry to debt-collectors in his province, he indignantly refused, even though this attracted the ire of Brutus and displeased even his friend Atticus; and he firmly kept to his announced policy of refusing to give a military post to any businessman (who would use it to extort whatever he wanted). At the same time, this same model governor did not hesitate to give a military post to a man going to the kingdom of Cappadocia to collect debts on behalf of Roman senators; and he naively explains that he can do this because it is outside his province. In fact, not only a prefecture, which was a fairly low officer post: he actually offered the man a military tribunate—which the man in the end did not take up, because he no longer needed it. Apparently the debt had been settled without his further promotion.[28]

Cicero prided himself on being old-fashioned in the discipline he kept. We may safely assume a similar difference in standards fifty years earlier. But it is hard to imagine the *publicani* simply organizing slave-raids into Bithynia: surely Nicomedes would have complained before! We have to assume (since he did not) that they were legally entitled to abduct his subjects; and that he merely brought the point up when the chance arose, in order to get it stopped if it were possible. The easiest explanation is that the *publicani* had lent the King money and he had offered some of his subjects for security: he was presumably the owner of all men not living in cities. Client kings were always desperately short of money and eager to borrow; and a little later we find a King of Egypt borrowing from Roman financiers and, in a way, pledging his actual kingdom as security.[29] It is revealing that they preferred investment outside the territory controlled by a Roman governor. Whether the *publicani* actually went in for slave-trading, we do not know. The words as reported by our source (for what they are worth: they are not good evidence on the original wording) certainly do not imply it, and it is doubtful whether the *publicani* had the specialized organization needed for that highly specialized business: it is easier to imagine that they sold the men off to some of the big firms centred on Delos.[30]

The Senate, obviously, was shocked: it is clear that they had not known what was going on. Their quick—even, as it turned out, rash—reaction proves it. Nor is this very surprising. Senators were not allowed to own estates outside Italy, or even to leave Italy without special permission; and probably very few of them had been to Asia and even fewer travelled into territory not controlled by Rome. We are entitled to believe that, nearly twenty years after C. Gracchus, *publicani* found it more profitable to act beyond the frontiers in order to act unobserved; and that, when found out, they had to submit to prompt control on the part of a Senate not in the least afraid of their reaction.[31] As I have observed elsewhere: it is nothing short of absurd, in the circumstances, to believe that this class could have been pressing for expansion of the Empire.[32] It is equally absurd to hold that C. Gracchus had aimed at putting the chief political power in their hands and making the Senate subservient to them—if he had, one can only say he had abysmally failed. But it is easier to believe that he had succeeded in what he aimed at: a system that was working markedly better than before his intervention.

However, within a few years things had deteriorated. By 95, things in Asia were going from bad to worse, and, with Mithridates threatening from outside and no doubt intriguing inside the province, the Senate again decided to take firm action and sent the distinguished jurist Q. Mucius Scaevola Pontifex, consul in that year, to look into what was happening and reform it. With him, to assist him, went another distinguished consular jurist (and philosopher), P. Rutilius Rufus, now in his sixties.[33] The appointments show that there was serious trouble in the province: no consul had ever been sent to govern a peaceful province, and no distinguished consular had ever served as a legate except in a major war. This time the objective was different: as we have noted, both men were upright, and both jurists. The results were strikingly successful. We have some evidence of Scaevola's activity: he tidied up the system of legal administration, recognizing the use of Greek judges (and Greek law) in cases concerning only Greeks; he reconciled two cities that were at loggerheads; he may have introduced the system of *dioeceses*—a generation later we find the province divided into districts, each centred in a major city, in each of which the Roman governor or his representative had to hold assizes. (The system is also found in other provinces, e.g. in Sicily.) We do not know where the idea came from or when it started; but there is no evidence of it before this time, and it is very likely that the eminent jurist, sent to reorganize an unhappy province, was responsible, as he undoubtedly was for the recognition of Greek law within the limits mentioned. His main achievement, perhaps, was his edict, which Cicero, in a different province over thirty years later, took as his model.[34] Cicero took from it, in particular, a clause that annulled—in polite and unobjectionable form—all contracts, including the *pactiones,* made contrary to good faith (e.g. through the use of force or threats—we have seen that this might be a necessary and useful provision).

It was at just about the same time that Ptolemy Apion of Cyrene left his kingdom to Rome by will. Nothing was done about it, and for a long time after this we do not hear of *publicani* there, even though it was undoubtedly a lucrative field for exploitation.[35] The Senate, as I have tried elsewhere to show at length, was always opposed to unnecessary annexation; and at this time it seems to have still regarded annexation as made necessary only by strategic reasons. But the striking failure to hand Cyrene over to exploitation reminds us of what was done in Macedonia in 167: we may well suspect that it is connected with the bad reports that had been coming in from Asia and that, at this very time, were making Scaevola's extraordinary mission necessary.[36]

By the middle of the nineties, therefore, although there are bad signs and portents in Asia—the province where the *publicani* were most powerful—it still looks as though the Senate was retaining firm control: no sign that the *publicani* are gaining political power by blackmail through the courts; and we must remember that there are more courts than before, by now, so that their chances might seem to be increased. The only real complaint one can bring against the courts in the nineties, however, is that they were so prone to acquittal that it seems to have become practically impossible to convict any senator.[37]

It can be confidently asserted that, when this turned out to be false and disaster came to the Gracchan settlement, it must have been a complete shock: we have no reason whatsoever to think that anyone, at this time, foresaw any danger from the new class that had, on the whole, given such a satisfactory account of itself in the judicial duties assigned to it. Politics in Rome, in the nineties, had proceeded according to the usual pattern, and we have no evidence of any appeal to the *equites*: the failure of such appeals by C. Gracchus himself and his successors may have taught Roman politicians a lesson.

But it was out of Q. Scaevola's distinguished mission that disaster developed. His work in the province had struck at the interests of many members of the new equestrian class. He had earned their hatred through this;[38] yet it was, in the end, not he who was attacked. It is to be presumed that, after a long series of acquittals, and (as we saw) no positive evidence that control of the extortion court had done much good, those who mounted the attack thought they had better not aim too high: the *pontifex maximus* might have overawed any jury.[39] Whatever the reason, it was his legate P. Rutilius who was the chosen victim. He was more vulnerable. First of all, he had actually stayed longer, administering the province for three months in accordance with Scaevola's rules, after Scaevola (who had no stomach for provincial life, any more than Cicero later) had departed—in order to save the province expense, as he put it.[40] Also, he was an uncompromising man, disliked by many, and he was likely—as indeed he did—to invite martyrdom. Defeat could not be risked, and P. Rutilius was a better victim. Moreover, we must add what is only to be expected in Roman conditions and what will appear even more clearly later: despite their control of the courts, the *equites* were helpless unless they had support in powerful senatorial circles. We have seen that they were not a homogeneous class—far from it. For various reasons, the *publicani* by now probably predominated on the jury panels; but one could not ignore the country squires, ready to submit to the *auctoritas* of the Senate and of senior senators, and with no 'class loyalty' towards financiers who happened to be their colleagues and equals. Now, it was in that class that C. Marius was influential. He—whatever the truth about his connection with the *publicani*, which may be no more than *ex post facto* invention based on this very incident—had risen from the class of country squires and could surely rally them. And he was an old enemy of P. Rutilius, glad to do him any harm possible; particularly as his own prestige was slipping.[41]

P. Rutilius' conviction was a scandal; and it would not have been possible without the help of Marius. But it was, first and foremost, a victory for the *publicani*, who had had their revenge and shown their power: the sources are unanimous that it was mainly they who had been restrained and punished during Scaevola's administration, and that they had been the chief offenders. For the first time, the Senate had lost the power of governing. The new class, which C. Gracchus had given power without responsibility, had shown that it could use that power irresponsibly, if not to govern the state (for that was not its purpose, nor in its power), at least to prevent it from being governed. We have seen that the behaviour of the *publicani* in the provinces had for some years been giving cause for concern: this is why the Senate had responded, in Asia and perhaps in Sicily and Cyrene, in different ways. But now a 'secret of empire' had been revealed, which no one (least of all the *publicani*, it seems) had hitherto even suspected: if they used their power with unscrupulous determination, they could do almost anything they liked. C. Gracchus is not to be blamed for not foreseeing it. Few of our own planners, with all kinds of electronic machinery, have proved able to foresee developments five years ahead, let alone thirty. It is important to recognize, in the light of the facts, that the danger inherent in his system of balance and the creation of a new class with judicial power took a whole generation to develop, and that even a few years before the explosion of the Rutilius trial, no one appeared to be able to guess it. In C. Gracchus' day, it was simply inconceivable that the right to govern of the Senate as a whole could be challenged: certainly, Gaius himself had shown no desire to challenge it—quite the opposite.[42] As far as the courts were concerned, the issue then had been the conviction of the guilty; and in this respect (as we have seen) he had greatly improved things. That the acquittal of an innocent senator could ever be in doubt was so much of a shock when at last it did happen that we can be sure it had not been expected or intended a generation earlier. But now the fact had to be faced: no one was now so innocent—or so powerful—that he could be secure.[43] Rome had become ungovernable. What is more: where a disgruntled member of the governing class (C. Marius) had shown the way, others now followed. A young enemy of the great Senior Senator at once seized the chance of prosecuting him, on a charge connected with Asia and sure to attract the interest of the very circles that had convicted P. Rutilius.[44]

The shock caused by the Rutilius affair called for quick reaction. The results were startling. The tribune M. Livius Drusus entered upon his brief moment of prominence, supported by two senior members of the Senate, who rallied the majority of that body behind him.[45] He propounded a programme meant to solve all the accumulated problems in the State, including those of the Italian allies (for whom he proposed citizenship) and of the law courts (which he hoped to transfer to a Senate enlarged by adlection of three hundred *equites*). It is significant that his most eminent supporters (M. Scaurus, the Senior Senator, and L. Crassus, the orator whom we have met before, as a champion of the Senate's cause) had been among the most active opponents of Italian enfranchisement, so that they were in fact among those chiefly responsible for the Italian crisis.[46] Their sudden change of mind documents as perhaps nothing else can the seriousness with which they (and others like them, at lower levels in the Senate) regarded the crisis caused by the trial of P. Rutilius.

If the State was to be governable on traditional lines (or, one might almost say, any conceivable lines), the irresponsible *equites* must be dealt with. M. Drusus propounded the programme of which we could perhaps see a hint in L. Crassus' speech of 106: the return of the People into allegiance to the Senate; there was now a further development: the People was to include the enfranchised Italians. They, as was clear, could no longer be kept out; and once in the body politic, they would be the majority of the future. As for the *equites*, some men in that order had (inevitably) shown political ambition. C. Marius was a good example; and during the years immediately following his first consulship several more 'new men' of equestrian origin (landed gentry, almost certainly: no breath of rumour links them, as it does Marius, with the *publicani*) had reached the consulship, and more still the Senate. The rush had subsided in the nineties. There is no sign whatsoever, any more than there had ever been, of a 'bid for power' on the part of the new class, such as modern historians sometimes anachronistically imagine. There had always been new men—ambitious and looking for support where they could find it. The disturbed conditions of the last decade of the second century gave some of them their chance of finding it in the People (though, of course, they would still need and get some support in the governing oligarchy). The picture of the *equites* as a class sweeping their leaders into power in order to govern Rome in their interest is absurd fancy.[47] If the Senate was—as seemed essential now—to regain control of the criminal law courts, its size would have to be at least doubled.[48] This provided an opportunity for raising ambitious men from the equestrian class to fill those seats. Once they were in the Senate, most of them would remain backbenchers, *pedarii* (lobby-fodder), whose voice would not be heard even to say 'Yes'. It is a fair guess that the total of the known men of ambition in that class would not surpass (or even reach) three hundred. Especially since elevation to the Senate would cut the new politician off from the public contracts and might seriously reduce his revenue, while greatly increasing his expenses: there were good reasons why some men at all times preferred equestrian status.

The leaders of equestrian opposition to Drusus—almost certainly *publicani*—would have nothing to do with a Senate seat. Of three mentioned by Cicero,[49] one (Cn. Titinius) was almost certainly of established senatorial family and could have got there before without trouble; C. Flavius Pusio is not heard of again; while

C. Maecenas is related to (if not identical with) Sertorius' *scriba*:[50] an office that, as we have seen, may not be unconnected with eminent rank in the public companies.[51] What they wanted was precisely to retain irresponsible power such as they had recently exercised.[52] In the end Drusus was overcome by the variety of interests he had offended: when his most vocal supporter, L. Crassus, died in mid-September,[53] his cause was lost; for M. Scaurus was too old and ill to play a full part in his defence. M. Drusus died; the Social War broke out, as the Italians saw themselves humiliatingly disappointed; and the victory of the *equites* was consolidated—with support from eminent senators like L. Philippus, who, as consul, had been chiefly responsible for Drusus' defeat—into a reign of terror against their senatorial opponents by the hallowed mechanism of a special court of enquiry: the emotionally powerful charge of having brought about the Social War made private vengeance socially acceptable. But it did not last long: it at once became clear that the equestrian class was not united, any more than it ever had been. Several prominent men (and perhaps some less prominent) were acquitted; and, with support from the People, the Senate finally succeeded in stopping the court.[54]

There followed the first civil war, with Sulla's march on Rome; and, after Sulla's departure, the victory of Marius and Cinna. The short period of the ascendancy of Sulla's enemies is described in a speech made under Sulla as 'the splendour of the *equites*'.[55] No evidence at our disposal justifies the phrase, which probably arose out of attempts to justify Sulla's bloody return to Rome in 82 as the victory of the nobles.[56] In any case, it proved very temporary, and after Sulla's return and bloodbath, the whole constitution was reorganized on lines that recall the programme of Drusus.[57]

For Sulla, trying to create a stable foundation for the republic, government by a strong Senate was the only answer.[58] The *equites* as a centre of power must (like others, e.g. the tribunes) be politically neutralized. To the method shown by M. Drusus, Sulla had a strong ingredient to add, that would assure success: the proscriptions, in which large numbers of *equites*[59] lost their lives or at least their property. With all possible opponents thus eliminated (and we know that he was more likely to err on the side of caution!), the raising of well over three hundred to the Senate must have been much more decisive than a decade earlier. There is no reason to think that Sulla confined his choice to *equites* in the old and strict sense, i.e. men who had the public horse. There would hardly have been enough of them, able and willing to accept elevation; and what we hear about the new senators does not suggest any such limitation.[60] In this, as in other respects, Sulla was not a reactionary: he accepted new developments (in this case the growth of the new class out of the Gracchan jurors) and used them for his purpose. It is most likely that it was he who cancelled the privilege of sitting in special rows of seats, which was 'restored' only in 67:[61] marks of distinction were the basis of power, especially in Rome, and power was just what the *equites* (in any sense) were not to have. Of course, he had nothing against *publicani* as such. They were essential to the State, provided they were—as they had been down to the nineties—kept under the control of Senate and magistrates. There is no reason to think that he took the lucrative Asian taxes away from them, as used to be believed;[62] or that their legitimate activities were circumscribed in any way. The State could not have done without them. And for the time being, his system worked well enough, restoring the balance of a generation earlier. In 75 B.C.[63] the Senate decided— no doubt for the sake of greater efficiency—to transfer the sale of Sicilian produce taxes (apart from that on cereals) to Rome, thus handing it over to the *publicani;* but after careful enquiry (at which a very eminent Sicilian was heard), the consuls decided that they should be let on precisely the same terms (those of Hiero's law) as hitherto in Sicily, even though those terms were apparently less favourable to the collector and to the State itself than the terms obtaining in other provinces. In 74 and 73, a complaint from Oropus, similar to the Pergamene complaint in 129,[64] was heard in Rome and finally decided by both the consuls of 73, sitting with a commission of senators that (as it happened) included young M. Tullius Cicero: the decision, as in 129, went against the *publicani.*[65] It was in 75 - 74, too, that an arrangement was at last made to collect the revenues of Cyrene,[66] since money was urgently needed in a grain shortage. This seems to have opened up a new field to the *publicani*: the Senate, at this time, was neither in fear of them nor prejudiced against them.

Sulla's surgery worked so well that we have no evidence for any political activity by the *publicani,* or indeed the *equites,* during the decade after his retirement. It is, of course, during this decade that we happen to have the revelations of the *Verrines*—which help to show us that there had apparently been no diminution in the scope given to the public companies, or in their rapacity (where they could get away with it). It is interesting to observe Verres' happy co-operation with Carpinatius, at precisely the time when a Senate commission was refusing to hand the sanctuary area at Oropus over to the *publicani*: clearly, once again, it was the behaviour of the governing class that made the system a good or a bad one; just as it had been the co-operation of members of that class that, even under the Gracchan jury law, had alone given the *publicani* their real power.

It was the governing class—Sulla's Senate—that brought about the disintegration of the Sullan constitution. It was, as might have been expected, a body of little moral authority, governing with a bad conscience.[67] The juries provided by the Sullan Senate were soon riddled with corruption, to such an extent that the age of the Gracchan jurors could be presented as a golden age. By 70, as appears from the *Verrines*, it was clear that the Senatorial juries had disgraced themselves. Cicero, for dramatic purposes, presents his case as their last chance to save themselves; but in fact, by the time the speeches were published, a law of 70 (passed by the praetor L. Aurelius Cotta) had already shared the juries between Senate and *equites*—not, as far as we can see (and we have plenty of evidence), owing to any demands by the *equites*, who, throughout the events leading up to the year 70 and the liquidation of the spirit of the Sullan constitution,[68] are, one might say, remarkably quiet. With their position of judicial power largely restored, the *equites* soon become a major political pressure-group—in every case where we have any evidence, supported and egged on by members of the governing class trying to use them (just as those same men and others tried to use the People) for their own political purposes. Within the equestrian jury panels, the *publicani* are soon back in their position of pre-eminence. They are frequently referred to in Cicero's speeches, and he even comments explicitly on the large number of them sitting on a jury.[69]

Cicero had foreseen this, when there was talk of restoring the *equites* to the juries. In a well-known (and often misused) passage, he makes it clear that, if the juries were in equestrian hands, they would be in the hands of the *publicani*.[70] We may ask: why was this so? We have seen that the equestrian order was far from homogeneous, at any time. Now as before, it must have had a solid backbone of Italian squirearchy—now even more so than before, since Italy had all become Roman. Of course, rural squirearchy was not entirely separate from financial interest: it has been shown that the great families of the Italian South appear to be represented among Roman businessmen in the East.[71] The public companies, in particular, must have attracted a large influx of new Italian capital. And this is probably part of the answer to our question: the *publicani* (i.e. the leaders of the large companies) dominated the equestrian order, on important occasions, because almost certainly interest and participation in the companies was widely distributed among the wealthier elements throughout Italy. Cicero's stress, in his speech on behalf of Pompey's appointment to the commands in the East, on the large number of Roman citizens interested in business operations in Asia, and on the interconnection between business and the tax companies, is no more than reasonable.[72] That interest was now spreading even further, as we shall soon see. Moreover, the heads of the large tax companies were, from the nature of their business, probably among the wealthiest of the *equites;* and they were also among the most distinguished, for social prestige within the order was intimately connected with birth and length of tenure of the rank, as was inevitable in Roman social conditions. Cicero's client Cn. Plancius had a father who was one of the leading *publicani*. His equestrian standing went back for several generations—probably as long as his native town Atina had had the full citizenship: we do not know when it attained that status—and his ancestors had been among the local squires of their town through the generations:[73] it is a splendid example of the kind of background that made the leading *publicani* combine wealth and social eminence into *gratia* and *auctoritas,* the mainstays of political power in Rome. We have already noted the Rupilii, a leading family of Praeneste.[74] If we knew more about the background of other great *publicani*, we should no doubt find the same. These men were closely related to senators, the families, in different branches or generations, passing in and out of the Senate: we have seen men like P. Rupilius (*cos.* 132), whose family retained interests in the companies, which appear generations later; Cn. Titinius, the *eques* opposing M. Drusus, probably to be counted a *publicanus,* and related to a minor senatorial family. A T. Aufidius was a small partner in the Asian company and later became governor of Asia.[75] The family is known among *negotiatores* (financiers) in the East in the second century; and at the same time there are senators with the *praenomina* Gnaeus and Titus, traceable at various times through the century.[76] Such men could justly be said to be linked to senators both by political favour and by *dignitas*—that seal of quality not usually applied except to senators.[77] One could sum it up by saying that the *publicani* (and this, of course, meant the leaders, not the ordinary *socii*, who were dismissed before important decisions were taken) were the flower of the equestrian class, an ornament to the State.[78]

Social and financial eminence together guaranteed political power. It was, as we have seen, not generally wanted, except for particular purposes. *Otium*—the pursuit of their interests, free from political danger and responsibility—was the desire of most *equites* (as Cicero often makes clear).[79] The ambitious, who were prepared to accept the expense and responsibility of senatorial status, could easily do so. Several are attested, and they usually had little difficulty, at least at the lower levels of public office. But they were obviously few, until a very late date, when (apparently) there was much less sacrifice involved and they could retain a good deal of their financial interests. But these men had more than eminence. Whatever their origin (often, as we have seen, in the country), they kept residences in Rome: their business interests necessitated it. For that reason alone, they were on the spot when jury lists were compiled, and more likely to be put on them. Also, as we have already noted, they were probably organized in some sort of professional association as early as the seventies, and therefore better able to bring pressure to bear. It is not at all strange that they are so often identified with the *equites* in our sources, when in fact we know that the *equites* were far from homogeneous in interests or opinions.[80] As we have come to see in our own time, it is the most vocal, the best organized, those with access to the centres of power, who come to be regarded as speaking for a class, whatever the evidence that a 'silent majority' of that class may hold very different views. When the *publicani* chose to act, they were a powerful force.

There is no doubt that they helped to put Pompey into the Eastern command against Mithridates, after L. Lucullus, like Q. Scaevola before him, had offended them by looking after the interests of the provincials in Asia. Needless to say,[81] they had to get the support of important senators: ultimately, it was the division within the governing class that gave them their chance, as it had in 92, and even in the second century. But that could now be taken for granted. It was a constant in Roman politics, waiting to be exploited. And it was the *equites* resentful at his Asian settlement who gave the impetus.[82]

That they had the support of many senators is easy to understand: not only for reasons of political faction, but for reasons of economic interest. As has recently been increasingly recognized, Sulla's reform of the Senate, flooding it with a majority from a non-senatorial background, had done much to obliterate the difference between the orders, helping to eradicate the stigma that attached to non-landed wealth—in this, as in other things, Sulla had shown himself thoroughly up to date. In the late (post-Sullan) Republic, senators shared financial interests with *equites* and— as was to be expected in view of their larger fortunes—outdid them. We know that, when Cicero had difficulties with unscrupulous moneylenders in his province, they were caused not by *equites* (who were only agents), but by the unspeakable M. Brutus; and Pompey owned much of the East that he had conquered.[83] It is to be conjectured—and it takes little ingenuity to do so—that the increasing hostility to L. Lucullus in the Senate, after 70 B.C. and his Asian settlement,[84] is to some extent due to the worthy senators who were hit in their own pockets, just as Brutus was in Cicero's Cilicia. *Concordia ordinum*—Cicero's constant dream—was, in the Ciceronian age, largely an accomplished fact, and largely at the expense of the provincials.

Pompey duly conquered and organized the East. The result was the greatest increase in the opportunities offered to the *publicani* since Gracchus' reorganization of Asia. Between his day and Pompey's, no other province (as far as we know) had had the Gracchan system imposed on it. In 70, certainly, Cicero could still give the impression that Asia was the only province with *censoria locatio* of its main tax in Rome.[85] Pompey added Syria, and reorganized Bithynia (adding part of Pontus to it), Cilicia and probably Cyrene. We have no positive proof that he introduced the Asian system there.[86] But it is likely because of the major and increasing interest the *publicani* henceforth have in Syria, and one can deduce it from indications in Cicero. The Bithynian company which P. Rupilius served[87] is simply 'the Bithynian company'; yet when we have references to companies farming grazing-tax or customs, we are explicitly told, in dozens of instances. In Syria, Gabinius' 'persecution' of the companies and their representatives is set out in horrifying detail: it includes the freeing from liability of many *uectigales* and *stipendiarii*.[88] Contrast Macedonia, where Piso equally persecuted that miserable class: there we hear only about interference with *portoria*.[89] We may take it that Pompey extended the Asian system to his provinces, and thus, at one stroke, multiplied the companies' opportunities. This may well have been one reason—though we have no details—why some responsible senators fought against ratification of Pompey's settlement—though there were so many others that one cannot be sure.

The settlement was ratified only in 59, through Caesar's action and with M. Crassus' support.[90] One ought to be able to tell the difference in the situation before and after. The civil war was soon to obliterate the effects; but a difference in scale at least comparable to that made by C. Gracchus ought to leave some noticeable effects. Above all, one would expect extreme shortage of capital. As we have seen, much of the actual capital of the companies—huge as it was—was tied up in their business: the amount of cash available was relatively small. Of course, the influx of the Italians into recognized citizenship and hence into the *publica,* since 70 B.C., had led to a great increase. It must have greatly increased competition for the contracts available; and, at a time when fighting was going on in the East, tax contracts there would be fewer and less profitable than usual. This helps to explain why, in 61—the first year after the victory over Mithridates when contracts were let, presumably by the censors of the year—there was frantic competition for the most lucrative of the contracts. Cicero thought it due to the publicans' greed; moderns tend to echo this, or to be baffled. But we ought to show a more mature understanding of simple economic causes, in our day.[91] In any case, the result was a considerable overbid, showing the strength of competition; which seems to indicate a healthy functioning of the system as a whole. For the first time since the elder Cato's censorship, we hear of a request to the Senate to lower the contract price—by no less than a third.[92] As so often, it was not the company concerned that had the temerity to raise this issue: the idea was strongly supported by M. Crassus, and (according to Cicero) came from him. M. Cato, no doubt recalling family history (and, in general, interested in good government), strongly opposed the petition, and kept it from being granted for over a year—with the result that the company, at least in the first year, had to go on collecting as best it could and recouping its anticipated loss at the expense of the provincials. Q. Cicero, governor at the time, must have found his life made much harder by this. Needless to say, his brother was strongly supporting the petition, despite his private disapproval: as he points out both to Quintus and to Atticus, his friendship with the *publicani* was a cardinal principle of his policy; and, of course, he honestly thought it in the public interest to maintain the *concordia ordinum* which, under the stress of common fear of Catilinarian revolution, he had managed to symbolize and to cement in his consulship.[93] As we have noted, there was a sufficient basis of common interests between Senate and *equites* to make such a hope more than a mere dream; and not only general interest in social stability, but particular economic interests. It is this solid basis that helps to account for the fact that the composition of the courts never again (after 70) became a matter of controversy between the two orders.

In fact, the division of function between actual government and State business was breaking down. It was only old-fashioned men like Cato who still fought to preserve it. That things had (at least sometimes) been different as recently as the seventies, when the Sullan system was still in working order, has been shown. We must, however, ascribe to the seventies and the sixties what made the major breach in the economic division between the two orders: the development of senatorial participation in the public contracts.

The phenomenon is attested, but not generally recognized. It must have developed gradually. As recently as 70, Cicero could allege it as Verres' most heinous crime that he had practically (never officially) been a *socius* in the public companies under his control:[94] 'the most serious charge that men can remember since the establishment of the extortion court'; and—as serious—Verres had known this was being said and had done nothing to contradict it, going so far as to suppress any public hearing on the matter. We do, in the seventies, find a consular as *praes* for a client's contract;[95] but this was a sacred contract, for the upkeep of the temple of Castor and Pollux; and we have seen[96] that there seems to have been a special exemption in the case of sacred contracts, which (probably) preceded the establishment of the prohibition as a general rule. In any case: Cicero's elaborate statement on the Sicilian case makes it clear that senators must have been excluded from tax companies: otherwise it would be impossible to ensure that the governor of a province and his senatorial staff were not *socii* of any company active in the province. Moreover, in all the cases involving companies that we hear of, there is never any mention of a senator as *socius*.

This state of affairs as such does not change, as far as we can tell. When various cases concerning companies are heard in the Senate—the petition of 61; and later the charges against Gabinius[97] —there is no question of any senator being actually a *socius* and speaking for the company in that capacity. It is merely evaded, and apparently on a large scale. As it happens, we know very little

about the details—as so often in what everybody knew and took
for granted. But we have one cardinal reference to it all in the
interrogation of Vatinius, which is so important that it must be
quoted in full: 'Did you extort shares, which were at their dearest
at the time, partly from Caesar, partly from the *publicani*?'[98] This
shows us various things, none of which we could have suspected
from any other evidence I know: that there were shares (*partes*)
in the companies, which appear to have had a kind of market
quotation (they were high in value in 59, because the tax-farmers'
request for a remission of one third was granted in that year);
that such shares could be bought either directly from the company
or from one who already held them; finally, and most surprisingly,
that both Caesar and (later) Vatinius held such shares. Rostovtzeff
long ago noted the 'Stock Exchange jargon', though he rather
exaggerated it; he quotes four phrases (three from this passage)[99]
and gives the impression of much better attestation than in fact
exists; he adds that this developed in the second and first centuries B.C., although in fact this passage only refers to 59 and we
have nothing earlier.

Partes (shares) in the public companies, of course, are as old as
the companies themselves. The word means no more than what
a *socius* had. The same applied to a private *societas*: Cicero's
speech for the actor Q. Roscius is full of discussion of the *partes*
of *socii* in a private *societas*. Similarly for the public companies.
When Cicero speaks of the large *partes* that his client C. Rabirius
Postumus had held in the public companies at an earlier time,[100]
he undoubtedly means that Rabirius had been a major *socius*; and
when he goes on to say that he let his friends have *partes* in his
affairs, it is not clear whether his private financial ventures (also
just mentioned) or his membership of public companies are meant.
Similarly, when we are told that a man called T. Aufidius had
held an *exigua particula*, a minute share, of the Asian public company, he must have been a minor *socius*.[101] This man, incidentally,
later became proconsul of Asia, and (says our moralist) 'those
allies who had seen him fawning on the tribunals of other men
did not disdain to obey his *fasces*'. (He turned out an excellent
governor.) It follows that he must have been in the employ of the
company in his early life, presumably in the province as *pro
magistro*. The passage is interesting because it suggests that that
official might have only a small share in the company he served
—unlike (presumably) the *magister* in Rome. But all the cases we
have considered are no doubt of regular *socii*. Indeed, the words

'socius' and 'particeps' go together quite regularly, even in their metaphorical meaning.

But the shares owned by Caesar and Vatinius seem to have been in a different category. The fact that they had a variable quotation and the fact that Vatinius extorted them from Caesar suggest that they were not the regular subscriptions of a *socius*, but shares traded 'over the counter', as Rostovtzeff thought. Nor —as we have seen—is any senator (Caesar, Vatinius or another) ever called *socius* of a public company. Indeed, had such a man been a *socius*, he would (under the Roman social system) undoubtedly have been a leading one and taken the lead in speaking for the company. As we have noted, there is every reason to think, in view of the total absence of open senatorial activity in the companies, and the explicit statements of exceptions, that senators were not allowed to be *socii* in them; and we remember that the magistrate letting the contract had a register of *socii*. However, I would suggest that the shares traded in 59, about which we get our incidental information, were *unregistered* shares: an obvious means of evasion, of a thoroughly Roman sort, if senators were to be interested in the public companies; and also, of course, technically very convenient (as in certain modern analogues) where the maximum freedom of trading is wanted both by the company itself and by those buying a financial interest in it. The incidental nature of our notice shows how ownership of such shares by senators was by then taken for granted, with no official stigma attached. (What Cato might have said is another matter.) For even though the manner in which Vatinius is claimed to have obtained his shares is painted as dishonourable, his possession of them is not; nor—even more decisively—is Caesar's. Indeed, it is Cicero's purpose, throughout the attack on Vatinius, to discredit that hostile witness *without* giving offence to Caesar—a very difficult feat; but Cicero repeatedly insists that he has no charge to make against Caesar and that Vatinius' case is on a very different level.[102]

We are fully entitled to conclude that these unregistered—and, presumably, therefore, 'non-voting'—shares were widely held by senators at this time, as indeed by other classes. They were by now obviously part of the structure of a public company, supplying an important part of its capital. It is excruciating that we do not know when this practice started. We are reduced to guesswork. Presumably, when M. Crassus egged the Asian company on to ask for remission of part of its contract price, he was not doing so for purely altruistic motives.[103] Presumably, therefore, senators were already interested in the companies in 61; as indeed one would expect from the fact that in 59 the matter does not call for comment. We may be certain, on the other hand, that this was not so in the days of Polybius: that careful observer could not have failed to mention this link between Senate and (as it was in his day) 'People', had it existed.[104] It may have started after C. Gracchus' law on Asia suddenly made far larger capital necessary for a major company. We have no evidence. But perhaps the history of occasional opposition between Senate and *equites* during the following generation suggests that there was no such community of interests. As we have to guess, the most reasonable conjecture seems to me to be that the custom came in some time in the seventies, under the less scrupulous rule of the Sullan Senate, when a large number of new senators had come to the House straight from association with the companies and (we may think) were not willing to forgo this source of profit altogether, just when elevation had greatly increased their expenses. At the very same time, with the failure to appoint censors in the seventies, and working censors after 70, the lists of members of the contracting companies perhaps simply came to be less scrupulously kept, allowing over-the-counter trading to develop.

Whatever precisely the origin of the system, its existence made an enormous difference. It meant that the traditional division of functions between government and public contracting was dead. Some senators—Cato, perhaps—still observed it, like other moral relics of a sterner age. But on the whole, Caesar and Vatinius—accepted without any surprise or disapproval—must be more typical. We may guess at some of the benefits that, e.g., Cicero—who always stresses his close association with the *publicani*—derived from his early forensic activity on their behalf; and what he meant by stressing (as he often does in letters of recommendation) that a governor who aided a particular company would 'find them most grateful'. These references have usually—and, up to a point, rightly—been regarded as political; but gratitude to Caesar and Vatinius had taken more concrete forms, and one may be sure that others could expect no less.[105] In fact, we may take it that this time the public contracts were a regular part—how large, we cannot tell—of many senatorial incomes. Of course, it is obvious that a man like Caesar or Crassus, owning even non-voting shares, would exercise quite disproportionate influence within the company; we have seen that Crassus was the one who put the Asian company up to its request for relief in 61. Much of the exploitation in which the companies indulged must have been connived at, or even directed by. senators, including some eminent ones. This, once recognized, is perhaps not altogether surprising. We remember that by this time senators—like Pompey and Brutus —were also the principal money-lenders in the provinces, probably using *equites* as their agents.[106] We can see once more to what an extent *concordia ordinum* was an accomplished fact, except for a few recalcitrant reactionaries in high places. By the end of the Republic, the principal business affairs of the *equites* must have been well on the way to being shared, if not taken over, by senators.

Senators, of course, had far greater capital at their disposal than *equites*, at least individually, if not collectively. This must have been particularly important when the organization of Pompey's new provinces again led to a vast increase in capital demands on the companies. We have seen how, before that organization was ratified, competition was massive, with too much capital bidding for too few contracts. Pompey—not unversed in business, as we well know—will have been aware of this uncomfortable economic fact, which must have had disruptive effects at Rome and even in the provinces in more ways than one. We cannot tell to what extent his decision to extend the Asian system to his new provinces was due to this knowledge; but, although there were perfectly good economic and political reasons for this step in any case, it is worth suggesting that this may have been one relevant consideration. And, to look at it differently, he must at least have been aware that the amount of capital awaiting investment was likely to be sufficient to cope with the vast increase in business—which, at a rough estimate, must have amounted to a trebling of the volume of tax contracting.[107] It is no wonder that in 60 the praetor Q. Metellus Nepos could carry—against the wishes of most of the Senate, it seems—a law abolishing *portoria* in Italy:[108] the contractors could afford it—and might even welcome it, since the collection of these tariffs, from vocal Roman citizens, was now hardly worth their while.

The effect of the ratification of Pompey's *acta* in 59—despite the law passed by Caesar granting the tax company of Asia its relief, well over a year after its first application[109]—was to produce a shortage of capital. No doubt, with peace restored (it must have seemed) for the foreseeable future, there would be plenty of new capital forthcoming in unregistered shares, if the *socii* did not want to see their control of the companies endangered. The contribution of senators, in particular, must (as we have already noted) have been very welcome at a time of shortage. In any case, the situation on the capital market was totally transformed—quite apart from the private fortunes made by the sudden increase in the market value of the shares of the Asian company.[110] As a result of these developments, and of the overbid of 61, which had taught the *socii* a severe lesson, we find the companies getting together into a cartel. There is no record of any State action against this, and it seems to have been done quite openly and officially. But henceforth there would be no more competition for the major contracts. (The small contracts were probably beneath the notice of the large companies and would not be affected.) Perhaps the authorities realized that only in this way could the shortage of capital be met and the vital contracts let at all; or perhaps this is simply further confirmation of the fact that most senators saw no reason to oppose anything that would secure the profits of the companies. But in the late fifties the new picture is quite clear.

We have noted the responsibilities of P. Terentius Hispo: *pro magistro,* in the same quinquennium, of the grazing-tax of Bithynia (hence Cicero's recommendation to the governor of that province) and of a tax in Asia, which implied a *pactio* with Ephesus. This was later defined for us by Cicero, when he describes Hispo as having been *pro magistro* in Asia for the grazing-tax and customs (*portoria*). It follows that during that quinquennium the same company held the grazing-tax throughout the vast area of Asia and Bithynia, and the customs in Asia as well. (Quite possibly in Bithynia too: we simply do not know.) We have seen how this illuminates the standing of Hispo himself. It would be interesting to know whether Cicero's Cilicia was also under the same company. We have a single reference to the company that farmed the two taxes (associated again!) of *scriptura* and *portorium* in his *dioeceses*: Atticus will be able to use their frequent mail service when writing to Cicero.[111] The reference to 'his *dioeceses*' ought to mean—as it does elsewhere—three districts of the province of Asia which had been attached to Cilicia;[112] and it is difficult to see why Atticus is particularly referred to the mail service of the company holding the two taxes mentioned in those three districts. Cicero, as it happens, never seems to refer unambiguously to the companies for particular taxes of Cilicia proper. And the mail couriers he himself uses, on one occasion, seem also to be those of the *dioeceses*.[113] It is not certain what conclusion we are to draw from this. But what it probably adds up to is that the three *dioeceses* were under a different company from the province of Cilicia proper: i.e., they were fiscally attached to Asia, even though at the time under the command of the governor of Cilicia; and that this company—the one managed, in the province, by P. Terentius Hispo—was a much larger one, with much more efficient services than the company (or companies) operating in Cilicia proper: Cicero is in fact telling Atticus that he will have a really first-class service at his disposal.[114]

The company farming these two taxes throughout (certainly) Asia and (probably) also Bithynia and the three districts detached from Asia and put under Cilicia was obviously a large and powerful organization. It was closely connected with Cicero. As it happens, we also learn something about the company farming the main tax (the tithe) of Bithynia—one of the two principal revenues (the other would be the corresponding tax in Syria) instituted by Pompey. In a letter recommending one of its agents he says that it 'consists of all the other companies' and forms 'a most important part of the State'.[115] (He also stresses his own close connection with that company.) It is thus that we learn one of the chief results of the events of 61 - 59 B.C.: it is clear that, in order to raise the vast capital required—and to avoid a recurrence of the unpleasantness of 61: the Asian overbid—the companies had got together, formed a joint company for the exploitation of the chief Bithynian tax, and—as this clearly implies—done away with genuine competition. There had been organization of a sort before, as we have seen; and *publicani* had felt loyalty towards one another as members of the same order. There were at least some who thought that one *publicanus*, in a legal case, should never decide against another.[116] But there had nevertheless been competition for the contracts; just as, even though manufacturers in a modern state will be closely linked in an association and defend their joint interests, yet they will normally be in competition with one another where their products overlap. What we find by 51, therefore, was radically different—as different as a cartel is from a manufacturers' organization or a Chamber of Commerce. And, as we saw, the cartel now, after a fashion, must have included the whole upper order of society and of the State, except for a few traditional aristocrats. Again, it is interesting that, in Cicero's surviving extortion cases (where he speaks for the defence, after the single prosecution of Verres in 70), the *publicani* always support the accused magistrate. We have seen in the case of Verres how a ritual expression of gratitude was now part of the accepted ceremonial on his return.

The situation has a certain similarity—though one must not press it too far—with the Marxian analysis of modern capitalism and its tendencies. This analysis, as is now known, did not sufficiently take into account the reaction of democratic societies, and the very influence of Marxist parties, in preventing the completion of the process. In Rome—if we may cautiously pursue the analogy —there was not only no real opposing force, but (as we have seen) there were in fact forces positively working *for* a quick concentration of the contract companies into a cartel. There was, however, no State machinery able to expropriate them and perform the whole of their vast operations. Instead, the immediate further development was typically Roman: it occurred to some senators and magistrates that the companies might now be cut out in individual cases and the profits got more directly—not, so far as we can see, for the benefit of the State, but for the benefit of the governor. Participation in the companies had given them an idea of the profits that might be got; and most had been content to co-operate and collect their share. Of course, unscrupulous governors had always had a large cut of their own. Verres showed what could be done by intervening in the sale of locally sold taxes; and, profiting by the vast independent powers of the governor, a man might even get away with introducing new taxes and apparently collecting them on his own authority—and, no doubt, at least partly for his own benefit.[117] By going shares with the *publicani* in the actual province, one could—as Verres had shown—increase profits all round; it is very likely that men like Cicero's predecessor Appius Claudius Pulcher in Cilicia had followed and improved upon this example. And one could make this more acceptable locally by letting selected members of the provincial upper class in on the spoils, as (again) Verres had done in Sicily and Appius did in Cilicia.[118] The politician—quite apart from having the governor's power—had something to teach the mere businessman in point of method. Most of these men—luckier than C. Verres, if only because they were active a little later—survived all attacks made on them at home and lived to reach positions of honour: Appius became censor in 50[119] and a leader of the party of the constitution against Caesar. But two men, of whose efforts to undermine this profitable co-operation and take the system over for their own benefit we happen to know through Cicero's hostility to them, perhaps took the lead in further development. L. Piso, Caesar's father-in-law, has already engaged our attention as one who, as governor of

Macedonia, knew how to make the maximum profit out of his provincial supply vote.[120] It was he who apparently managed to set up his own customs station in the port of Dyrrhachium, through which most trade between Italy and Macedonia (and some other areas) passed.[121] Later—if we are to believe Cicero, as on this specific point we well may—he instituted a fixed sales tax in the whole province and collected it through his own slaves,[122] thereby (no doubt) seriously undermining the profits of the company that had purchased those particular taxes. His ex-colleague as consul of 58, A. Gabinius, as governor of Syria, went further still. It is difficult to gather the facts that underlie Cicero's almost hysterical ranting against him: such charges as that he handed over the poor *publicani* to the natives; that he refused to hear their cases in court; that he refused to admit any of their agents into a city that he visited or was intending to visit; that he overturned many fair *pactiones* and illegally exempted many subject communities from tax; finally, that he even drove many innocent *publicani* not only into bankruptcy, but into death.[123] But it must (as is widely recognized) amount to major and systematic interference in the whole system—to nothing less than an attempt to undermine it. It would be pleasant to join those modern scholars who, from dislike of the *publicani* and their methods, claim that Gabinius felt genuinely outraged by what he found going on and tried to relieve the provincials of the burden. But nothing in what we know of his character entitles us to such an attribution of altruism. Some of his actions, undoubtedly, were due to political hostility either to the *publicani* as a class (they had supported Cicero in 58, when Gabinius had helped to procure his exile, as Cicero never ceases to remind us) or to individual men or companies: thus, we do not know what they thought of his military operations (for which he was refused a *supplicatio*).[124] But there can be little doubt that he himself derived the major profit from his actions, as indeed later on from his intervention in Egypt.[125] If the revenue was perhaps somewhat reduced, at least he seems to have collected it all himself; and we do not know how much of it ever reached the Treasury. Needless to say, the *publicani* were now his bitter enemies, and they found support among members of the senatorial class; as a result of which, despite Pompey's half-hearted efforts to save him (for he had loyally served under Pompey earlier in his career), he was ultimately exiled:[126] one of the very few provincial governors after Verres to be convicted as a result of his actions in his provincial command.

In fact, he had shown the way, as Piso also had. The companies had built up a system that was ready to be taken over. Integrated into the State and working in co-operation with it and (on the whole) with members of the ruling oligarchy, who shared in the profits and must have indirectly run some of the organization, they had undoubtedly done their essential job of collecting the revenues. But they had always—and especially since C. Gracchus—been an irresponsible class in a position of at least occasional political power. Gracchus had set up a business class consisting of the traditional *equites* (accustomed to provide the leaders among the *publicani*) and the rest of the wealthiest non-senatorial citizens, and had tried to turn them into a constitutional check on the oligarchy, which would enable it to do its work of governing more satisfactorily. When, a generation later, it was clear that that class threatened the whole fabric of government, Sulla—after various solutions had been thought of—restored power to a Senate enlarged by a major injection of that same class—in fact, a numerical majority. The result was indeed to make the new class politically impotent and restore Senate ascendancy; but the Senate itself was now pervaded by the outlook of the class from which most of its members came. The traditional division between public business and public administration (including the supervision of that business), which C. Gracchus had never challenged and which his reform had in fact intensified to the point of a serious split, now began to crumble. Add to that the low morale of the post-Sullan senators, taken largely from the class whose political irresponsibility had precipitated the crisis that led to the Social and Civil Wars, and consisting entirely of those who had welcomed the rebellious proconsul and deserted the government of Rome[127]—and it becomes clear that the outlook for the Sullan system was not good. During the seventies, the Senate gradually lost its authority and that public acceptance on which its rule was chiefly based; while fear of the Sullan veterans surrounding Rome began to fade. With Pompey, largely for personal reasons, adding his weight to the popular agitators, and M. Crassus—the only other leader who had emerged with an enhanced reputation from the late seventies—deciding to join him rather than defend the system they had both helped to instal, the year 70 saw, suitably (in view of the Verres scandal), the restoration of the Republic, including the restoration of the *equites* to the criminal courts, which they henceforth shared with senators.

That restoration at once converted them—and, among them,

chiefly the leading *publicani,* distinguished in wealth and in organization, in birth (on the whole) and in closeness to the centres of power—into a major political force in the state. No new leaders emerged, to take the place of those crusty old *publicani* who, in 91, had fought on behalf of the irresponsibility of their order and had disdained exchanging their status for that of a minor senator.[128] With the polarization between Senate and *equites* a thing of the past, and senators now—as we saw—able to keep up a highly profitable connection with the public companies, *equites* are willing enough to enter the Senate, or at least to let their children do so, for increased *dignitas* and power.[129] This is what lays the foundations of that *concordia ordinum* (understanding between Senate and *equites* in defence of their common interests) which Cicero made one of the foundations of his policy, and often (especially in the Catilinarian troubles and in the agitation for his return from exile) with fair success.[130]

On the famous occasion when the *publicani* asked for remission of the Asian contract,[131] the conflict only confirms the rule, and helps to deepen our insight. They were supported (and, Cicero thinks, put up to it in the first place) by M. Crassus, who undoubtedly must have been a large shareholder, if (as we saw) Caesar was in 59. It is clear that, even if not a voting member, let alone a *magister,* an eminent senator connected with a company was bound to have a great deal of influence in it. Cicero, in accordance with his general political principles (we cannot prove that he had any shares), also supported the application. There seemed to be little opposition, except from the consul designate Q. Metellus Celer and (it was thought) from Cato. So far Cicero. We learn from a scholiast (and it may well be true, since Cicero's comments in the *Pro Plancio* help to confirm it) that the whole matter was later talked out, chiefly owing to Cato's efforts. Even as late as 59, over a year after it was first raised, Caesar (then consul) was unable to get the matter settled in the Senate and finally took it to the Assembly. It was apparently on an occasion when the filibuster was being used that the elder Cn. Plancius lost his temper and made some remarks more characteristic of old-fashioned freedom of speech than of tact. In any case, it seems that a small noble clique was able to block a decision—and prevent what we may confidently assume would have been a favourable vote— by parliamentary tactics. The small circle of traditional-minded noble families, in fact, seems to have acquired even greater authority and power in the Senate and in elections through the enlargement of both the Senate and the People in the preceding thirty years. The case of Cicero's client Plancius brings a strange revelation: when a new man defeated a noble, even for an office of medium rank, he had to fight a presumption that he had used illicit means. Cicero takes this so seriously that it is clear his audience (senators and *equites* forming the court) also did. 'All of us who are good citizens favour the nobility', he was to say on another occasion.[132] The history of his age shows that, on the whole, it was true, particularly for the wealthier citizens who decided elections and the outcome of trials. At no other period of Roman history could a noble tribune elect have swung the whole house to his opinion—he would probably never have got as far as speaking.[133] The power of M. Cato in the Senate points up the political ineffectiveness of the mass of new 'equestrian' senators, whether the remnants of Sullan adlection or even of recent consular standing. *Concordia,* as Cicero frequently makes clear, meant the acceptance of noble political tutelage. As a result, the *publicani* incongruously turned to demagogues and the mob for the attainment of their limited objective, which the great majority of the Senate would gladly have granted them.

The affair of the Asian contract did not cause a split between the Senate and the *publicani*—indeed, as had been the case ever since C. Gracchus, the demagogues earned little gratitude. It was a young leader of the *publicani* (himself a future senator) who took the lead in supporting Cicero when he was threatened with exile in 58,[134] and the public companies joined the Senate in demanding and welcoming his return in the following year.[135] Such men had no permanent love for the mob and its leaders; even though they objected—as Cicero himself did, when he dared to say so—to the aristocratic arrogance which, as far as they were concerned, alone stood in the way of *concordia*. They and their relatives in the House were willing enough to follow the political lead of the nobles: they had no policy of their own, and the policy of international brigandage that had become characteristic of some of the political leaders suited them well enough.[136] Their active intervention in politics was limited to their own immediate interests; and there they had come to expect co-operation, and would take it wherever they found it. Pompey had been their champion, to whom they owed vast new business opportunities, not to mention (indirectly) the accommodation over the Asian tax remission; yet a majority thought nothing of joining his political enemies to convict Gabinius, who had set the dangerous precedent of exploiting a province for his own benefit.[137] It was thus that they were once more turning out to be an element making for instability, and preventing purposeful administration and the reasonable treatment of Rome's subjects, on which the future of the empire might ultimately depend.

There is no doubt that some governors stood in awe of them: one has only to read Cicero's remarks to his brother in his famous letter on provincial government;[138] or to read Cicero's speeches for the defence of various men accused (all of whom—in the surviving speeches—were supported by the *publicani*). We might, however, keep things in perspective. It is easy to say that the *publicani* were the scourge of the provinces; one tends to forget about the governors and their senatorial subordinates. There is, in this period, no second Rutilius scandal: Gabinius amply deserved what he got (and it took two separate charges to convict him). On the contrary: the exactions of the *publicani* would become bearable under good governors, intolerable only under bad. We have seen how much power the governors had to make things worse: Verres had turned an acceptable system of mild exploitation into a nightmare. He obviously had successors. L. Sergius Catilina in Africa was patently guilty of many charges, and escaped only through a collusive prosecution.[139] It is clear from his electoral failures— long before he turned revolutionary—that the *ordo publicanorum* had no great love for him. The facts concerning Cicero's Cilicia are better known than most: the intolerable exactions of the vile Ap. Claudius are amply substantiated in detail; and his equally aristocratic predecessor, P. Lentulus Spinther, appears to have been no better:[140] at least, we know that he, like Appius, used to receive 200 talents (over a million denarii) each year from the cities of Cyprus (annexed to the province) alone for not billeting the army on those cities.[141] In the circumstances, the cities were hopelessly in debt, i.a. to the noble Brutus.[142] We need have no doubt that Cilicia itself had been treated similarly: on Appius, we have explicit testimony. One result of this was that the *publicani* had not been able to collect. It seems that they were in the habit of fixing punitive interest for late payment in their agreements (*pactiones*);[143] this had no doubt added to the hopeless indebtedness that Cicero describes on his first arrival in his province: Appius' exactions had left nothing over and plunged the cities into debt, and the governor obviously had first pick of what money could be raised.[144] Such punitive interest, though possibly illegal,[145] had been recognized as valid by governors of the province ever since the seventies.[146] However, the situation that Cicero found was that there was simply no money to be got: things seemed to be at a dead end, and the *publicani* had, at least in some cases, not been paid for five years (i.e. during the governorships of Appius and, before him, of Lentulus Spinther)—not even the interest, let alone the principal.[147] Cicero took two steps to deal with this. First he investigated local accounts and found—as he expected—that large amounts of public money had been embezzled by the magistrates, clearly with the co-operation of the governors. We remember Verres, and his sharing the booty with selected members of the local upper class;[148] Cicero also remembered. It was (we may gather) standard form, for a certain type of governor. In any case: the local men were persuaded to repay what they had taken, and the cities paid all their arrears. This, however, was greatly helped—if not made possible—by another measure he took: he announced that he would allow interest only at the legal rate of 12 per cent per year laid down in his edict, provided they paid by a certain date; if they did not, he would recognize the punitive rate of their agreements (probably nearer 48 per cent, which was what Brutus charged his provincial debtors).[149] By means of these two measures he seems to have managed to get the cities' accumulated debts cleared during the short time of his administration.[150]

This in itself suffices to show how great the influence of the governor was, for good or ill. A succession of noble governors, collaborating with the local hierarchy of office in enrichment at the expense of (inevitably) the poor, had reduced the province to a state in which the civic finances were hopeless, with neither taxes (except those the governor collected for his own pocket) nor interest being paid. Yet an honest and tactful governor cleared it all in six months or so. As the Salaminians told Cicero in another connection: they were really paying out of his pocket, since he was not demanding the money that governors had customarily demanded.[151] The *publicani,* admittedly, were out for what they could get; they had no political responsibility. But we now see that they might not in fact get very much, because others were ahead of them in tapping the supply.

Now, what was their reaction to Cicero's arrangement? We know that L. Lucullus—not to mention P. Rutilius Rufus—had been attacked by them for reducing the burden of debt in Asia. What about Cicero, who had cheated them (they might think) of a fortune in interest charges—on paper? The surprising fact is that they did *not* think so. They were happy. Cicero, of course, was an old and trusted friend, not a supercilious aristocrat like Cato. That made a difference. Moreover, he quite possibly had a personal stake in the companies concerned (especially that served by Hispo). He flattered them and treated them with the honour and consideration they expected, but did not always receive.[152] Granting all this, we may still feel surprised that they were happy. No doubt they had come to realize two facts, in the preceding years: first, that what they did not take today might not be available tomorrow;[153] and secondly, that they could no longer count on a governor's taking them into partnership: the governor might find it more profitable to take the local aristocrats into partnership (practically) at their expense, as Appius had done, and no doubt Gabinius.[154] The *publicani*—perhaps late in the day—were learning their essential weakness.

This is almost the last we hear of them, under the free Republic. The wheel was coming full circle. As we saw, the interests of senators and *equites* (including, most prominently, *publicani*) in the post-Sullan Republic had become very similar, promoting a natural *concordia,* which was disturbed only by the behaviour of a few old-fashioned aristocrats. In some cases this behaviour may have sprung from political morality; one might give Cato the benefit of the doubt. In others (and perhaps more commonly) it was the kind of noble arrogance (*Appietas* and *Lentulitas,* as Cicero calls it)[155] that did not go with any moral superiority; thus L. Domitius Ahenobarbus, whose insults stung the spokesman of the *equites* on the matter of Gabinius into a rude reply, was involved, together with Appius Claudius, in the notorious election scandal of their consular year.[156] Brunt rightly stresses the desire of the *equites* for the recognition of their *dignitas*:[157] their attachment to Cicero will to some extent be due to the fact that he lavishly recognized and proclaimed it. A small incident is illuminating. Bibulus, in his provincial edict, had included a clause not recognizing contracts entered into in bad faith. This irritated the *equites* (particularly sensitive to charges of bad faith, as of corruption), and Atticus expressed that irritation to Cicero. Cicero, as he himself tells Atticus (obviously expecting him to be fully satisfied), achieved the same effect by a more tactful wording.[158] Again, we must agree that the *publicani* (and the rest of the equestrian order, as far as they were politically active) were not simply unreasonable. In a world run by openly corrupt aristocratic politicians, they had every right to object to being singled out, one might say, as scapegoats. The story of Cicero's dealings with the *publicani* (and others) in his province helps, if not to redeem them, at least to put their attitude in the right perspective. They did not write the rules of the game, and naturally complained if the rules were written in such a way as to hurt them and gain illegal profits for the writers. They obviously played their part in exploiting the provincials, as they had a generation earlier. But we do not (as in Asia in the nineties) have a fairly simple picture of equestrian exploitation, with the Senate trying to keep it under control. The political code of the late Republic had made the *publicani* more reasonable and less dangerous. What had begun (after Sulla) as a partnership in exploitation was inevitably producing a new difference between the partners. The real exploiters were the governing élite, armed with power that had itself now become irresponsible. The *equites,* in the field of public contracts as in other areas of business, had consolidated their power and organization, only to find that they had to be content with the leavings. They cannot fairly be blamed for the disintegration of political morality in Rome or in the provinces.

The Civil War reinforced the lesson. Sulla had shown long ago that those who had arms and were prepared to use them were the masters of those who had mere wealth. Wealth, as M. Crassus had implied, was no use unless one could arm a legion. The losses suffered by the *publicani* were once more immense.[159] Their provincial offices, which must have contained the bulk of the money passing through their hands, were emptied by one army after another; and it is to be imagined that their property (their capital investment) was not spared.[160] Naturally, their own exactions increased in proportion: it was only human to pass on part of the burden to those weaker than themselves, when they had the chance. We need not doubt that the complaints about them in Asia, on which Caesar acted, were fully justified. But once more, it was not they who had written the rules of the game being played; even though they were the objects of conspicuous odium, and obvious scapegoats for the events in which they themselves had been caught up. Caesar, we are told, helped the cities of Asia by abolishing the farming of the basic tax of Asia—thus reversing what had been the first step in their real greatness.[161] The burden of taxation is said to have been reduced by a third[162]—a piece of what must originally have been Caesarian propaganda, which we cannot fully interpret.[163] Whatever the truth, the cities no doubt paid less, and paid it to Caesar's agents without the help of *publicani*—precisely what, according to Cicero, they had at one time not been able to do with the levy imposed on them by Sulla.[164] It was, presumably, a more refined form of a practice that we have had occasion to observe before: a combination of Roman ruler and local aristocrats to share the profits made out of their own peasants, cutting out the *publicani*: Caesar had learnt from Gabinius. Yet there is no reason to think that Caesar distrusted the *publicani* in principle. Asia remained a special case. The system of by-passing them was not extended. Caesar, for one thing, could do it in one province, as Gabinius had; but he still lacked the large central office staff to adopt the system throughout the empire. *Publicani* remained an integral part of Roman tax-collecting machinery until well into the empire: in fact, much more is known about their detailed organization at that time than at the height of their power.[165] Caesar (who, until towards the end of his life, was well informed and had sound political judgment) knew by experience and observation what we have noted in our analysis of Cicero's relations with the *publicani* in his province: it happens to be the only case we can analyse in detail; but although Cicero was no doubt exceptional in self-conscious rectitude, he will hardly have been unique, and the perceptive contemporary observer could not fail to make the analysis that even we can reach. Caesar knew that, for all the clamour about oppression by the *publicani*—which he would exploit when it suited him—the real oppressors were the rulers of Rome; and for all the fear of the *publicani* as a political force, what mattered was control of the State machinery, which he intended to retain. Treated with courtesy and assured of their reasonable profits, the *publicani* would co-operate without a murmur.

In fact, Caesar cheated them—and the Roman Treasury—of another source of revenue as well: he gave away Cyprus to the Ptolemies.[166] Yet he did nothing to humiliate the order, not to mention the *equites* as a whole; and we may imagine that he treated its leaders with the aristocratic courtesy characteristic of him at his best. As for the leading *equites*, it is well known that he created major opportunities for them—as other Roman aristocrats had done on a lesser scale—in his own financial and political service, thereby preparing their future use as an administrative class. Men like Matius and Oppius might well have been—and perhaps in fact were—'founders of the largest public companies, directors of many'.[167] They regarded Caesar's trust and friendship as more important.

Apart from Asia (for Cyprus was a matter of high policy),

Caesar did nothing to show any suspicion of *publicani*. No doubt he regulated their activities by law (perhaps even as early as his first consulship of 59), just as he had those of senators.[168] There is no murmur of protest. Private enterprise was to continue for a long time to serve the Roman State, with no more dishonesty than its public servants, and in co-operation with them. At the same time the prestige, the *dignitas,* of this important task faded away as the equestrian public service attracted ambition and commanded respect in its place.[169] We never again hear of *publicani* as the ornament of the State, the flower of the equestrian order, linked to the Senate in *dignitas.* The problem of the tax-farmers, about which so much had (and has) been said and written, turned out (not surprisingly, perhaps) to have been the problem of the Roman oligarchy itself, without which the *publicani* had never (even in the nineties) had any power or political leverage. The taming of the oligarchy removed the problem. Rome discovered, in the end, that the key to the problem of private enterprise in the public service —*any* public service—lies in those who govern and in the principles and practices of Government. The power of mere wealth was, and is, a myth. The issue of whether public or private services were to be used for a given purpose faded into the background. It can be exciting enough as an issue, or a political diversion; but it is ultimately irrelevant, particularly to the governed.[170]

Notes

I

Contracts in Peace and War

1 Luke 5,27f. and 19,1f.; Mark 2,16f.; Matthew 9,9f.
2 See, e.g., T. Frank, *Roman Imperialism* (1914), 320f. See M. Rostowzew [= Rostovtzeff], *Geschichte der Staatspacht* (*Philologus, Suppl.* IX 3, 1902), 479f. (also illustrating their wealth and power).
3 Livy xlv 18,4.
4 *Q.fr.* i 1,32 'quibus si . . . omnibus in rebus obsequemur, funditus eos perire patiemur quorum non modo saluti, sed etiam commodis, consulere debemus.'
5 Contrast the emotive force of such terms as 'modern' and 'progressive' (or 'old-fashioned' and 'reactionary') with that of Latin 'nouus' (e.g., but not only, in 'res nouae') and 'antiquus'. In the Roman social context, it must have seemed much more emotionally satisfying, for anyone who thought of himself as a man of character, to vote against a new bill rather than for it: the formula of rejection ('antiqua malo') was one that, as a general principle, most serious-minded Romans would have approved.
6 F. Kniep, *Societas Publicanorum*, i (1896—all published). This work still contains much useful discussion on the legal technicalities concerning the public companies. (The reference is to p. 92: Jena

contrasted with Weimar. Though Kniep himself favours direct collection, he is inclined to make an exception in the case of the road-tax: it seems the German government had been finding it difficult to control the civil servants collecting it!)

7 J. P. V. D. Balsdon, *The Romans* (1965), 33.

8 In general, see still N. D. Fustel de Coulanges, *The Ancient City* (frequently reprinted) ; the original *La Cité antique*, appeared in 1864: especially useful in stressing the religious foundations, which nowadays tend to be overlooked ; W. Warde Fowler, *The City State of the Greeks and Romans* (1893).

9 Ulpian in *dig.* xxxix 4,1,1 'Publicani . . . sunt qui publico fruuntur, nam inde nomen habent.' Though a little later he confines the term to the contemporary meaning of public tax-collectors. Kniep, 1f.

10 This is commonplace for students of early Roman history. See, e.g., P. G. Walsh, *Livy* (1961), chapters II-VI ; my own essay in T. A. Dorey (ed.), *The Latin Historians* (1966) ; A. H. McDonald, in *Fifty Years (and Twelve) of Classical Scholarship* (1968), 465f.

11 E.g. Juno Regina (v 23,7) ; Salus (ix 43,25 ; x 1,9) ; the *Villa Publica* (iv 22,7) ; city walls (vi 32,1).

12 Pliny, *n.h.* x 51 ; Livy v 47,4 (the exact date does not matter).

13 Varro, *l. L.* vi 92. Again, at least an early Republican date is certain. See E. S. Staveley, *Historia* v (1956) 75f. (accepting a regal date) ; Sumner, *JRS* 1970, 77 (denying an early date for its Classical form, but accepting an earlier form).

14 Asc. 93 Cl. Cf. Livy xxiv 18,10 (discussed below).

15 K. Latte, *Röm. Religionsgeschichte* (1960), 248, gives references.

16 For this law debarring senators, see Asc. l.c. (n. 14), stressing the exceptional nature of permission. The contract for keeping sacred buildings in repair is closely associated with that for furnishing the sacred horses and chariots (Livy, l.c. (n. 14)). It is not surprising that in the first century we find an ex-consul associated with a client's bid for this contract. (Cic. 2 *Verr.* i 144, 150. This will be further discussed in ch. V.) Nicolet (*L'Ordre équestre* i (1966), 330) doubts, in view of that passage of Cicero's, whether senators were excluded from all involvement in contracts ; but, as we shall point out in greater detail, the absence of senators' names among the larger *societates* (public companies) that we meet in the late Republic is conclusive evidence for legal exclusion. These (and other?) *sacred* contracts were legal exceptions.

17 Livy xxiii 48,5f.

18 Livy, l.c. Not 21, as Ürögdi, *RE,* s.v. 'publicani', col. 1193.

19 Livy probably wrote most of his surviving books as he read the sources, never reading far in advance of his work. For his frequent

self-contradiction, and failure to do anything about it, see Walsh (n. 10 above), 141f.

20 Livy xxv 3,9f. (213/2 B.C.).

21 Livy xxv 1,2f.

22 Livy xxv 3,15.

23 Nicolet, 322f., denies this, apparently only because it is not explicitly attested. It can be taken for granted in both cases. Toynbee (*Hannibal's Legacy* ii (1965) 352f.), greatly exaggerating the impact of the whole affair, shows an alarming lack of awareness of Roman social niceties by claiming that M. Postumius of Pyrgi may have been a recently enfranchised Etruscan, 'at heart a Caeritan nationalist [*sic*] whose resentment against Rome . . . had not been appeased by his acquisition of the status of a Roman citizen *optimo iure*.' He cannot find anything of this kind to allege about Pomponius of Veii ; though the idea of the two fraudulent *equites* (one a Roman commander, the other related to a Roman magistrate) cheating the Treasury in a kind of Etruscan nationalist 'guerrilla warfare' has its charm.

24 Livy xxiv 18,10f.

25 We must remember that at this time (late third century) the only senior magistrates (with very small staffs under them—only a handful of men in each case) were 2 consuls, 2 praetors, 4 aediles and—once in a quinquennium—2 censors ; junior magistrates—10 tribunes and (probably) 8 quaestors, with a few minor magistrates rather poorly attested—make up the whole executive machinery apart from army officers ; and the consuls, praetors and some of the quaestors were, in varying degree, occupied by military duties as well.

26 The technical term for such contracts, '*ultro tributa*', is frequent in Livy and will at times have to be used, for brevity. See *RE*, s.v.

27 Livy xxvii 10,11f.

28 The text is corrupt (see OCT, *ad loc.*), as figures unfortunately often are. Out of the 4,000 lbs of gold, the two consuls and three other commanders were to get an equal amount each, which the manuscripts variously transmit as 'quingena' and 'quinquagena' ; and one of the consuls an additional 100 lbs for Tarentum. 'The rest' was to be used for the contracts. Since 'quinquagena' is absurdly small, 'quingena' is usually read ; this makes the sum distributed 2,500 + 100 = 2,600 lbs., and the rest 1,400 lbs. But Mommsen (*Röm. Staatsr.* iii 1097, n. 2) suggested that *both* figures should be read, 'quingena' having dropped out before 'quinquagena'. This would make the sum paid out 2,750 + 100 = 2,850 lbs, leaving 1,150 lbs for Spain. It is not a point on which I should care to decide. Weissenborn-Müller *ad loc.* accept Mommsen's reading and in their note give the 'rest' as the sum based on the other reading, i.e. 1,400 lbs!

29 This again cannot be known for certain, this time owing to Livy's incompetence and unreliability (see Gelzer, *Kl. Schr.* iii (1964), 220f.). See the table of legions in *CAH* viii 104, trying to follow Livy and assuming 4 legions for Spain. (Two consular armies might be expected to have at least that number ; and cf. Livy xxvi 19,10, with 17,1, giving 16,000 men.) But Livy xxvi 28 lists 17 legions for 210, yet speaks of 21 as under arms. One legion he has not included is later found in Greece (xxvii 7,15), and this suggests he may have had 3 in Spain in his sources. In xxvii 22,11 (208 B.C.) there is no longer a legion in Greece, so that there may now be 4 in Spain. This is only a small indication of why no exactitude can be claimed for our calculations. On the other hand, we have no reason to disbelieve Livy's explicit mention of the contract for the clothes (xxvii 10, *fin.*), and Weissenborn's comment *ad loc.* ('ohne Vermittlung der publicani'), with a reference to the fraud of five years earlier, is unacceptable. Frank appears to accept it, since he does not mention the contract under 'The knights' corporations' during the Hannibalic War (p. 102). It is difficult to imagine the quaestors letting contracts directly to producers, as this must assume: since there was no large-scale industry, it would involve a large number of small contracts, and the magistrates cannot have quickly established the necessary trade connections. The phrase used of this particular deal ('uestimenta . . . locanda') should, as usual, refer to *publicani*. It must be mentioned in passing that the cost of clothing was deducted from the soldiers' pay: the State could expect to get its money back in due course.

30 I have calculated throughout at the 'Classical' rate of conversion of 1,000 denarii to the pound of gold (Frank, 47). The figures are in any case not precise. Frank (102), in calculating—according to no real criteria—the value of the contract of 215, arrives at an investment of 1 million denarii for the *whole* deal and regards the investment by each of the 19 as 'trivial'.

31 Plut. *Cat. Mai.* 4.

32 For the size of legions see Pol. vi 20,8f. We should bear in mind Sumner's warning (*JRS* lx (1970) 67) that the figures are the paper strength, not necessarily the 'practical effective'. On the other hand, the full wartime strength was often 5,000 nominal (Pol. l.c. *et al.* ; Livy xxvi 28,7 *et al.*).

33 On the legions taken to Spain in 218 see Gelzer, l.c. (n. 29 above). Livy xxii 22,1 reports another 8,000 in 217, not making it clear whether they are Romans. (And see Gelzer's general warning, l.c.) The figures for the census classes will be found in any handbook. I have accepted (with most scholars) Mommsen's interpretation (*Staatsr.* iii 249f.) of the evidence. It is possible that a different standard for the *as* (the basic coin in which the figures for the

census classes are expressed) should be adopted, which would yield figures $2\frac{1}{2}$ times these for the classes (but this would not affect Equestrian census). A soldier's annual basic wage, right until Caesar's time, was 120 denarii: out of this he had (at this time) to pay for his food and clothing. (This is the figure commonly accepted. It has been questioned in recent years (see G. Watson, *The Roman Soldier* (1969) 89f., with references to his own work and other scholars'). But I see no convincing argument for their complicated theories, abandoning the usual equation of drachma and denarius in Polybius and other Greek writers. See Brunt, *PBSR* 1950, 50f.)

34 As the word suggests, it was probably collected through the organization of the tribes, by officials called *tribuni aerarii* ('Treasury tribe officers'). See however Mommsen, *Staatsr.* iii 227f., dissociating it from the tribes (it is not clear why: the *aerarii* were presumably thus called because they paid directly to the *aerarium* and did not belong to tribes; from this it does not follow that those citizens duly in tribes did not pay through the tribal machinery—if anything, the very opposite seems to follow).

35 Frank, 101. For the institution of the tax at a time of stringency, see Livy vii 16,7.

36 See S. J. de Laet, *Portorium* (1949) 45f.

37 There is an immense literature on public land (*ager publicus*). The subject can be adequately traced, in English, in Frank. For a standard treatment, see G. Tibiletti, 'Il possesso dell' *Ager Publicus'*, *Athenaeum* xxxvi (1948) 173f.; A. Burdese, *Studi sull' Ager Publicus* (1952).

38 On Flaminius, see sources cited *MRR* i 225. I adopt Frank's interpretation, p. 102.

39 Livy xxix 37,3.

II

Expansion and Conflict

1 The military establishment is discussed in Frank, 142, with further references.

2 Frank, l.c. Toynbee, 652, estimates about ten legions per year, roughly the same figure.

3 Frank, 149f.—based, as far as I can see, on Weissenborn-Müller (see ch. I, n. 29). Brunt, 138, briefly disposed of this. Unfortunately Toynbee (356) has now come out on Frank's side and the matter needs renewed (and longer) discussion.

4 xxxvi 2,12 ; xxxvii 2,12 ; 50,9f. ; xlii 31,8. Toynbee adds one or two passages, also dealing with grain ; especially xliv 16,1f.: Q. Marcius Philippus requisitioned grain from the Epirots, against a draft on the Roman government. He does recognize that the other requirements are farmed out to contractors (Livy, l.c.), but fails to draw the obvious conclusion that, while the Roman government, like all other ancient governments, was in the grain business, at least to a certain extent, it was not to any extent in the clothing or horse trade. It is entirely a matter of traditional connections and lines of business communication. Even so, private business had its place in the grain trade (n. 6).

5 Livy xxv 15,4 ; 20,3 ; xxvii 3,9 ; cf. ii 9,6 ; 34,3f. ; iv 25,4 ; 52,5. All missed by Frank.

6 Livy xxxiv 9,12. He sent them home, with the characteristic remark: 'The war will feed itself.' Clearly, like most things that Cato demonstratively did after this fashion, it was an exceptional step.

7 The machinery must be stressed: as we shall see, it was the chief contribution of the *publicani* to supply it. Since at this time—as archaeology has confirmed—there were no large 'factories' capable of coping quickly with an order such as the one we are about to discuss, the task of collecting several thousand garments (say) in a short time was one that required connections and expertise such as the government simply never acquired, or thought it its duty to acquire. In 205, only Etruria seems to have any major industry (Livy xxviii 45,13f.).

8 Ch. I, n. 31.

9 Frank 195, 200.

10 See ch. I, n. 33.

11 Frank, 138.

12 Unfortunately Frank tries to fix an 'exchange rate', which makes the sums he calculates quite misleading in modern terms. It is totally impossible to convert ancient into modern prices or incomes ; and anyone who has tried to do this for *contemporaneous* cultures with widely different living patterns (e.g. the U.S.A. and a typical underdeveloped country) will never attempt it. All one can do is to illustrate what could be bought (in the widest sense of that word) for certain sums at various levels ; and we have tried to do this.

13 See Mommsen, *Staatsr.* i[3] 241 ; iii 1109. (Though the details are not all clear.)

14 Livy xl 46,16 ; xliv 16,9. Brunt (139) rightly points out, against

Frank, that this is a large portion of the public revenue. It remains to be added that the payment is probably not isolated (see text). K. Gast, *Die zensorischen Bauberichte bei Livius* (1965), has nothing relevant.

15 See *MRR* i 404.

16 Livy xxxiii 42,10; xxxv 10,12 (193 B.C.); 41,10 (192 B.C.).

17 Frank, 149f.; 152. Again this is repeated by Toynbee (357), despite Brunt's decisive objections (139).

18 E.g. *ILLRP* 449 (an early road); 39 (' . . . aid(iles) d(e) stipe Aesculapi faciundum locauere eidem pr(aetores) probauere'); 45 (' . . . aidiles curules moltaticod dedere esdem probauerunt'—this just as in Livy). This last building appears to be early second century. Brunt's reference to *ILLRP* should be corrected: read (probably) '466'. He does not notice the aedilician inscriptions, directly relevant to Livy. It is slightly inaccurate to say (Brunt, l.c.) that 'In every case the person who had the "cura" of the undertaking had the "probatio" ': the Puteoli law (which Brunt cites, in support, from *FIRA*; a better text *ILLRP* 518) in fact shows the opposite state of affairs: the building there is commissioned by the duumvirs and approved by a council of twenty local senators. Cf., for a perfectly normal case (except for the way it developed!), Cic. 2*Verr.* i 130: it seems that, in routine work, if the work outran the term of office of the commissioning magistrate, his successor might be appointed for the *probatio*. But this may not have applied to new buildings (see *ILLRP* 39, quoted above). None of this uncertainty of detail, of course, affects the principal point: that all these works were *ultro tributa,* duly farmed out.

19 Van Nostrand, *ESAR* iii 128f.; the figures are quoted 129. It is not clear whether the idea was Frank's or his colleague's; but probably the former, as it fits into his (mistaken) general theory of 'distrust' of the *publicani*.

20 Brunt, 139 (citing D. Kienast, *Cato der Zensor*). Even Toynbee is doubtful, in this case (360); but he asserts (on the strength of Cato's presumed dislike for 'the new Roman business men') that 'the lessees will have been local'. Since no change in arrangements between Cato's organization and the time of Polybius (see below) need be assumed, none should be. Cato, at this time, had had no quarrel with contractors.

21 Frank (154) rather arbitrarily ignores the implication of Livy that the figures are booty. For the figures, see Van Nostrand (n. 19 above). The first three of the series show the randomness that best fits in with interpretation as booty (plus, perhaps, some 'voluntary' contributions by the natives): *206 B.C.*: 14,342 lbs of silver; no gold; large number of silver coins; *200 B.C.*: 43,000 lbs of silver; 2,450 lbs of gold; no coins; *199 B.C.*: 1,200 lbs of silver; 30 lbs of gold; no coins. Such variation is quite typical.

If the figures for 200 and 199 really include the mining profits (which would inevitably be a major part of them), mining operations must have been very haphazard.

22 Livy gives 10,000 lbs of silver and 5,000 lbs of gold for 174 (xli 28,6). At even a 10:1 ratio between gold and silver, these figures are large by previous standards—four years after Frank's posited 'reorganization' and the consequent exclusion of mining proceeds! Hence the 5,000 lbs of gold have to be emended to 50 (Van Nostrand, l.c.; some 'statistics' are based on this). There is a genuinely low figure for 168.

23 See *For. Cl.* 120f.

24 Livy xxxiv 21,7. Brunt (l.c.) rightly believes Livy and regards this as the first institution of contracts for the mines. He ignores the possibility of local leasing (as posited by Toynbee) and rightly rejects any opposition by Cato to the *publicani* as a general principle.—Salt was organized at the same time (see next note).

25 Fragment 93 (Peter)—overlooked by Brunt, it adds decisive support.

26 Had the mines been exploited in the Roman interest before 197 (at any rate), the decision to establish the Spanish provinces would not have had such a startling impact on the natives—or, to put it differently, the major revolt would have come sooner. (See *For. Cl.,* n. 23 above.) Since the Romans would no doubt realize this, it is very probable that they did not risk exploitation until their minds were made up on the general question of what to do with Spain.

27 Diod. v 38,1 (generally agreed to be from Posidonius): underground working day and night, until they collapsed. Cf. 36,4.

28 Strabo iii 2,10.

29 Pol. iii 59,7. (See Walbank *ad loc.*)

30 Even the slaves, however cheap, are a considerable total investment. There is no point in guessing (as Frank does) the 'writing-off' figures for the labour force. Though if we *had* to guess, nothing could be more absurd than his figure of 10 per cent per year—implying that those slaves, in those conditions, could live for ten years after starting work. One year would perhaps be a better guess. The futility of compiling statistics based on mere guesswork is shown by comparing Frank's figures for the investment and profit with those in *RE, Suppl.* iv, col. 146, s.v. 'Bergbau'. They are, respectively, 26 and 45 million for investment, 12 and 7 per cent for profit! I have tried to use no independent figures that do not have some source support and to stress the limits of that support: the mania for quantification where the evidence does not permit it is as disastrous to history as to economics and other 'social sciences'. Brunt rightly eschews this game (138f.); but his own statement that the contracting business 'may well

have yielded profits far greater than could be obtained from land' is in the same class. It may equally well have yielded much less. Cato the Elder certainly knew all about the possibilities. Yet in his work on agriculture (*agr., praef.*) he considers only trade and usury as more lucrative than farming (although in other ways less desirable!)—no mention of the contracts. We are entitled to assume that profit margins, at this time, were low. The equation of high turnover with high profits is often made by the demagogue; it should find no place in historical works.

31 Livy xxxix 44,7f.; cf. Plut. *Cat. Mai.* 19, referring especially to extensive building work.

32 Plut. l.c.

33 Brunt is right in drawing attention to the large scale of building work in Rome, which came the way of the contractors (139). One may confidently add a *private* building boom, as these same people adorned their houses and villas. The building was probably handled by much the same people and firms, whether on private contract or on public. The attested pressure of competition for the public contracts suggests that profits (in view of the scale of operations and, at times, laxer control) might be larger than in private work. There is some ambiguity or confusion in Brunt's remarks about work commissioned by generals (see, e.g., Livy xliii 4,6f.).

34 See n. 14 (above) and text. In 174—with major building stressed by the sources (*MRR* i 404) and no major war being fought—we may safely assume a repetition of the grant of one year's revenue made in 179. In 169, with a major war on, it was cut to half.

35 Livy xliii 16,2f.

36 Livy xliv 16,8.

37 Livy xli 27 (with gaps). Most of this building was done on the initiative of one of the censors, without official instructions; but the action seems to have gone unchallenged. The money must have been voted before; what was new was merely the way of using the grant. In this (as in other things) the censors always had a good deal of latitude.

38 He stripped a famous temple of its roof-tiles—an action officially disavowed, and punished by the enraged gods (*MRR* i 404). It does not, of course, follow that he was lax in his attitude to contractors.—We must remember that by 169 there had been another war on, for several years. It may be that—like the Hannibalic War—it had produced some scandals.

39 See the standard works, e.g. *CAH* viii 273f.

40 It is from the Senate debate on this that I quoted Livy's remark (p. 12 above): 'Where there is a *publicanus,* there is no effective public law and no freedom for the subjects' (xlv 18,4).

41 In fact, the commander on the spot (with the consent of the

Senate Commission) slightly modified the decree, permitting the exploitation of the (less important) copper and iron mines by Macedonians: the rent they had paid for this was halved (Livy xlv 29,11). Gold and silver mines in the hands of Macedonians were no doubt regarded as too dangerous (as seems to be Toynbee's thought (360, with notes), in a confused discussion). This same motive makes it almost certain that, when mining was resumed, it was handed over to the *publicani*: neither distrust of the natives nor the inability of the government to manage such matters directly had changed in those years. (*Contra* Brunt.) The Spanish precedent would prevail. (Toynbee thinks it most probable that they were handed back to Macedonians.)

42 Pol. xviii 35,4: see Walbank's note *ad loc.* for other figures, not all claiming to refer to the same event.

43 xlv 40,2f.

44 The Second Macedonian War had ended only in 196.

45 Frank, baffled at the Senate's generosity, thinks the Macedonian mines must have been exhausted (156). In view of the revenues that had accrued to the kings, this is hard to believe. In any case: what about the other sources of profit that were neglected? The fact that the mines were given up helps to disprove Frank's idea that the Spanish mines had been handed over to the *publicani* only in 178: the Senate clearly knew of no other practicable way of managing mines.

46 Livy xliii 16,1f.

47 Once we accept the connection Livy makes, we may safely add the further conjecture that the particularly harsh treatment meted out to the equestrian class (stressed Livy, l.c.) was closely connected with the misbehaviour of the *publicani*: presumably individuals guilty of whatever scandal had been uncovered were deprived of their horses.

48 Plut. *Paul.* 38, *fin.*

49 Livy xxxiii 42,10 ; xxxv 10,11. The view that there was no charge for use of this land at this time is erroneous.

50 Livy xxviii 46,4-5 ; xxxii 7,3. Frank (150f.), again followed by Toynbee (356), argues that the public land cannot have been managed through the *publicani*. The alternative conclusion is more likely: for reasons sketched in the text, they did not succeed in collecting.

51 Livy xlii 19,1f.

52 Some of the leading *publicani*, being *equites*, may, of course, themselves have profited by this failure to collect the rent ; this would allow the state of affairs to continue.

53 It seems that some of the land illegally occupied was even bought back, to avoid offence. The episode is not clear (Gr. Lic. 9 F).

54 Cato, fr. 167 M, regards senators' dislike of the law in 167 B.C.

as a matter of course, and the impact appears to be recent. But the date is not known. (Toynbee, 555f., is right on the *prima facie* interpretation, but adds romantic embroidery.)

55 Attested only by Cassiodorus 616 M.

56 On the time of composition of Book vi, see Walbank, *Hist. Comm.* i 636 (with references to detailed discussion).

57 Pol. vi 17. (Some of the technical terms connected with the public contracts were obviously difficult to translate into Greek.)

58 Walbank, *Hist. Comm.* i 692f. (though he relies too much on Frank's interpretation).

59 Walbank, l.c.; Brunt, 119 ('by the people he *of course* means the Equites' (my italics)).

60 Toynbee, 343. The contractors themselves, we are told in the same breath, 'were conscious that, in their perpetual "cold war" with the Senatorial Establishment [*sic*] it was they who had the whip hand.' It is a pity that that massive work, based on so much study of modern scholarship, comes to the evidence with a mind fully made up and much more attuned to recent than to Roman conditions.

61 I have translated the word ἐργασία as 'business'—one of its most common meanings. (It means 'activity', of any—especially any profitable—sort.) Walbank, following Mauersberger (*Polybios-Lexikon*, s.v.), translates 'profit' and refers to iv 50,3 ('Gewinn' (Mauersberger)). But there is no need to take the word in this specially made up meaning, in that passage any more than here: 'business' or some such word is as obvious there as here; and the fact that the word is plural does not necessitate a radical change of meaning. In v 100,4 it clearly means 'work'. Both Shuckburgh and Paton render 'work' in vi 17,3.

62 See the convincing article by H. C. Boren, 'The urban side of the Gracchan economic crisis', *AHR* lxiii (1957-8) 890f. Archaeology seems to be confirming the growth of the country towns of Italy at this period: a point readily forgotten in discussions of the antinomy Rome/'country'—e.g. by Brunt, *JRS* lii (1962), 69-86, which needs modification.

III

The Rise to Power

1 Val. Max. vi 9,8. (See *RE,* s.v. 'Rupilius', no. 5.)
2 See A. E. Astin, *Scipio Aemilianus* (1967), 84, 88f.
3 Frank, 262.
4 Toynbee, 362.
5 This concept of the *equites,* made familiar by H. Hill, *The Roman Middle Class* (1952), was rejected by most of Hill's reviewers. See, most recently, Wiseman, *Historia* xix (1970) 77. Brunt, rightly rejecting the view of the *equites* as 'businessmen', and as rightly stressing their desire for high social standing and recognition, in the late Republic, seems to over-emphasize their ambition for office (120) and comes near to implying a 'class war' of the sort imagined by Toynbee.
6 This distinction has been rightly stressed by Nicolet in his monumental work on the *ordo equester.*
7 I have tried to explain the working of this system and to stress its importance in preventing the creation of a caste society in my 'Marius and the Nobles' (*DUJ* xxv (1963-4) 141f.).
8 This truth, long recognized by careful scholars, has now been amply demonstrated in detail by Nicolet. It is less true in the late Republic than earlier, but still largely valid.
9 Cic. *off.* i 151.
10 Diod. xxxiv/xxxv 38.
11 Plut. *Mar.* 3.
12 Livy xl 51,2.
13 See ch. II, n. 61 and text.
14 A partial one in Pliny, *n.h.* xxxiii 141.
15 Front. *aq.* i 7 ; see Astin, *Scipio Aem.* 108f.
16 *MRR* i 474.
17 No major new building is recorded down to 125, except for Callaicus' temple of Mars some time after 138 (the architect was the famous Hermodorus: Nepos, fr. 20 P): see Boren, *op. cit.* (ch. II, n. 62). I would add the same Hermodorus' *naualia* (Cic. *de or.* i. 62).
18 For the story of Tiberius Gracchus, one of the most frequently treated in Roman history, see D. C. Earl, *Tiberius Gracchus* (1963) —stressing the political and military motive at the expense of the economic and the philosophical ; Brunt, *Gnomon* xxxvii (1965) 189f., upbraiding him for it and stressing the social and economic factors ; Nicolet, *REA* lxvii (1965) 142f., looking for a philosophical Greek background. I have written about it in the *Festschrift* for J. Vogt (forthcoming).

19 *The Failure of the Roman Republic* (1955). Appearing at a time when discipline and social cohesion still tended to be associated with Fascism, this work got what now seems an unfair reception from its critics. The loss of *concordia* in modern societies will perhaps lead to a revaluation.

20 Plut. *Ti. Gr.* 16. We need not discuss the question of whether the assembly at which he was killed was an electoral or a legislative one. (L. R. Taylor, *Athenaeum* li (1963) 51f., thought it was legistive; Earl, ibid. liii (1965) 95, denied it; Taylor, ibid. liv (1966) reasserted it.) Even if it was legislative, the legislation is not necessarily that of Plutarch. I have discussed the matter in my forthcoming article cited n. 18.

21 Pliny, *n.h.* xxxiii 34; Dio xxiv, fr. 83,7. For a different point, cf. Vell. ii 2.

22 Cited Plut. *Ti. Gr.* 8, *fin.*

23 See fr. 17 M; cf. 31,6; 47.

24 Cic. *rep.* iv 2.

25 On all this see Astin, *Scipio Aem.* 245 (with n. 1).

26 I tried to analyse a case on which we are comparatively well informed in *Mél. Renard* (1969), 55f.

27 Nicolet, *L'Ordre éq.*, 513f., wants to move the law down to come after the *Lex Repetundarum*. Though I disagree, he deserves thanks as the first recent scholar to stress the importance of this law.

28 Cf. *rep.* i 31 ('two senates and almost two peoples'), etc. It is not enough to say that he merely wanted Scipio as his hero. Historical probability took precedence. (Cf. *Att.* xiii 32, *fin.*: the subject came first, the persons have to be fitted into it according to historical plausibility.)

29 The consul P. Mucius Scaevola, who refused to act against Tiberius, later defended Scipio Nasica's action against him (Earl, *op. cit.* (n. 18) 117f.). This is not inexcusable.

30 Livy, *per.* lix. For the membership, see *MRR* i 495, 503.

31 App. *b.c.* i 19, 78f.

32 Cic. *Mur.* 40 ('restituit', 'restitutus', of the law in 67 that conferred this privilege on the *equites*). Other sources *MRR* ii 145. I cannot accept Wiseman's interpretation of Cicero's words and rejection of Vell. ii 32, 3 (*Historia* xix (1970) 80).

33 Senators had had their separate seats since 194 (see Mommsen, *Staatsr.* iii 519f.). Only conservative senators no doubt disapproved of the mark of *dignitas* for the *equites*; the People, who disapproved in 67, were not yet a real political force, least of all if the step was taken by a *popularis*. But it is possible that there was some conflict: a very badly preserved fragment of Obsequens (28a), to be placed in the years 129-127, mentions M. Fulvius Flaccus as triumvir, apparently in connection with *dissensio in legibus ferendis*.

34 See *For. Cl.* 176f.
35 This is sometimes denied, by those who think the landmarks of history can be obliterated by the tracing of origins. Origins are interesting and important ; but the landmarks remain and should be recognized.
36 The trial is probably to be dated 125 or 124, after his triumph, which was in November 126 (*MRR* i 509).
37 This is made abundantly clear by his law on consular provinces—perhaps the most significant piece of legislation for anyone interested in his political ideas. (Sources Greenidge-Clay², 37f.) He not only left to the Senate the most important administrative decision of the Roman year, but made it the only administrative act exempted from the tribunician veto.
38 I hope I demolished it *AJP* lxxv (1954) 374f. But it keeps reappearing in obscure places, based on the same misinterpretation of Plutarch. See n. 65 below.
39 See *For. Cl.* 216f. ; Gabba, *PP* xi (1956) 363f. ; *ASNP,* s.2, xxxiii (1964) 1f. On Sulla, see my Todd Lecture *Lucius Sulla* (Sydney, 1970).
40 Sherk, *RDGE,* no. 12.
41 Line 21 shows that the Senate decree was passed at the end of June. The other consul, C. Sempronius Tuditanus, was back to celebrate a triumph by October 1st (*MRR* i 504). The consuls must have been ready to leave almost at once after this important decision.
42 Line 15 mentions the revenues from Asia (presumably as being farmed out, as usually restored ; there is no indication whether in Rome or locally). Since we know that Ti. Gracchus wanted them for his agrarian schemes (see *For. Cl.* 174), this need not surprise us: the royal properties would become the property of the Roman People. The inscription, by implication, adds the knowledge that the contracts were let to *publicani,* hence (it seems) at Rome. Yet many scholars, for a long time, refused to accept the date 129 (which now seems certain—see Sherk, l.c.), on the ground that it was only C. Gracchus who introduced the *publicani* to Asia! The decree does not tell us precisely what was being farmed out at Rome. Certainly not the taxes of the cities, which remained independent under the royal will. Cicero tells us (2*Verr.* iii 12) that *censoria locatio* for these was instituted by a *lex Sempronia,* which must be one of C. Gracchus (Cf. App. *b.c.* v 4, 17, claiming that the tax was at first not collected by Rome, until 'demagogues' made it necessary.) This still leaves a good deal to collect. The dispute was precisely over the boundaries between city land and royal land (lines 5f.).
43 The contract had already been let, and only the company stood to gain or lose. But, of course, future prices for the contract would

be affected.

44 Sources Greenidge-Clay[2], 4f. The figure 1,000 (in the Livian *Periocha* and the book *de uiris illustribus*) is probably based on no more than a mistaken source. Our reliable tradition unanimously gives 500 *iugera,* about 300 acres. Corrupt figures are common in our manuscripts and will have occurred in those available to late sources. See my discussion *op. cit.* (n. 18, above).

45 We know of others later. See, on Oropus, p. 95 above.

46 Presumably through the *tribuni aerarii;* but Mommsen denies it. See ch. I, n. 34.

47 Plaut. *Trin.* 794; cf. the *scripturarius* of *Truc.* 144f. (guilty of illegal seizure). Toynbee (362), trying to show the power of the *publicani* in the early second century, misuses Plautus' references to *argentarii* for the purpose. They are quite irrelevant.

48 *Men.* 115f. A customs inspector also in Ter. *Ph.* 150. It should be mentioned that we do not know for certain when Plautus' plays were produced, since the tradition on him is confused and unreliable. None of the plays referred to are necessarily earlier than 200. It may be that the *portitor* was all the more amusing (and excruciating) because new.

49 De Laet, *Portorium* 55f. (with sources), suggests that tariffs were charged there before; but if so they can only have been local. This is the first Roman one. The text (Livy xxxii 7,3) appears to name another place, which cannot be identified. The new *portoria* seem to be part of a slow reorganization of public finance after the disaster of the Hannibalic War.

50 Livy xxxiv 45,1 (194 B.C.).

51 Livy xl 51,8 (*portoria* and *uectigalia*). This no doubt greatly increased the sum at their disposal for building, since they would let the contracts themselves and (presumably) appropriate one fifth of the purchase price for their projects.

52 Vell. ii 6,3. Cf. *ORF*[3], p. 188; Cic. *Tusc. disp.* iii 48.

53 See de Laet, chapters III-V.

54 De Laet, 97f.

55 Exactly as happened, according to Cicero, in the case of the tax on produce other than cereals (*2Verr.* iii 18). The original *lex Hieronica* must have provided for (individual) *portoria.* The *sex publica* of Cic. *2Verr.* iii 167 have been much discussed. They must include the *portorium* of Syracuse, for the *pro magistro* Carpinatius worked for a company that had farmed both the *scriptura* and the Syracusan *portorium* (*2Verr.* ii 171). Hence it is probable that they were all *portoria.* Rostovtzeff (391f.), comparing similar phrases found at a later time in Africa and Illyricum, suggested that there were six districts comprising the whole of the *portoria* of Sicily. Scramuzza (*ESAR* iii 340f.), noting that Cicero mentions eight Sicilian ports and refers to others, thought the six were

merely six out of whatever number of *portoria* there were, with the rest in other hands. This is accepted by de Laet (68f.), who adds the suggestion that they may have been six ports in what had been the kingdom of Syracuse, with the old Carthaginian part under a different administration (cf. the two quaestors). Calderone (*Kokalos* x-xi, 1964-5, 76f. = *Helikon* vi, 1966, 15f.: the articles are identical!), contrary to Cicero's explicit statement about tax arrangements in Sicily, wishes the *sex publica* to be the land of six cities confiscated (after revolt) by Rome and farmed to *publicani* at Rome. (He ignores the fact that the port of Syracuse is demonstrably one of the six *publica* concerned.) Calderone needs no further consideration. As between Rostovtzeff and Scramuzza, no certain decision is possible ; but the phrase 'sex publica' certainly sounds as though it was a fixed legal term and not a chance collection for a single contract term. Also, Cicero's list of eight ports and reference to 'cetera' (ii 185) is meant to stress Verres' opportunities for 'free' exports. It is not an administrative canon.

56 Pol. vi 17, discussed ch. II, *ad fin.*

57 The abolition is attested by Plut. *Paul.* 38 ; Pliny, *n.h.* xxxiii 56 ; Cic. *off.* ii 76. Toynbee (344) comments on the greater efficiency of the public companies as compared with the Roman government (adding that the latter deliberately maintained an inefficient constitution in order to maintain the power of the 'Establishment'). Yet he believes that the government, by letting the companies collect taxes, lost 'a substantial margin of its revenue'. This seems to rest on no more than the old fallacy we discussed in ch. I: that public management is *necessarily* more (or at least no less) efficient that private. This naive view has been shown to be only of limited validity in our modern world. For the odd view that Romans after 167 paid no more taxes, see (recently) Meier, *Res Publica Amissa,* 68.

58 See p. 60 above.

59 I have discussed the importance of this step, in purely financial terms, in *RILR* 47f. (with notes).

60 Plut. *Pomp.* 45 (based on Pompey's own statement) gives the Roman revenue from the provinces before Pompey's organization ; it was at this time that Cicero (*l. Man.* 14) emphasized the overwhelming importance of Asia.

61 See n. 59.

62 *ORF³*, pp. 181-2.

63 It is unlikely that the profit margin of the *publicani,* at least as originally envisaged, would exceed the amounts that tended to disappear into the pockets of Roman magistrates and their subordinates. There is no reason to think that the provincials would pay more, or the Treasury receive less, than under any

alternative system. Cf. ch. IV, n. 67.

64 It has been suggested (Rowland, *TAPA* xcvi (1965) 361f.) that
C. Gracchus was trying to restore the 'balanced constitution', as
described by Polybius, which might seem to have broken down.
Theoretical influences on C. Gracchus are certainly not to be
flatly disbelieved. Nicolet, in various works, has thoroughly investigated them.

65 The details of the law or laws by which he did this have been
much discussed. See, i.a., my view in *AJP* lxxv (1954) 374f.;
Brunt, 141f.; Gruen, 80f., 293f. Gruen rightly opines that 'the
quest for novelty continues' (one might add: as in other fields).
Gruen's own view is unacceptable, since he simply discards—
without being able or willing to explain it—the evidence of Plutarch and the Livy *Periocha* (p. 296: 'too confused to be at all useful for reconstruction'—i.e., not by any means to be fitted into his
own!). But the fact that in the end senators were replaced by
equites (in some sense of that term) is too well attested to be
denied by anyone.

66 That the inscription called the *Lex Repetundarum* (*FIRA* 7) is the
Gracchan law is now generally recognized; which is not to say
that someone will not soon be found to deny it. (See Gruen's
remark on novelty, quoted last note.) After centuries, we now
seem to have an acceptable text of this important law by H. B.
Mattingly, *JRS* lix (1969) 129f.

67 Mommsen changed his mind about this; which shows how difficult
a decision is. Nicolet firmly opted for the public horse. Wiseman,
Historia xix (1970) 78f., does not seem to commit himself.

68 Pliny, *n.h.* xxxiii 34: 'iudicum autem appellatione separare eum
ordinem primi omnium instituere Gracchi . . . mox debellata
auctoritas nominis . . . circa publicanos substitit . . . M. Cicero
demum stabiliuit equestre nomen . . . .' This must mean that what
later became the *ordo equester* was first set up by the Gracchi as a
class called 'jurors', then the name was applied to the *publicani*
[who, as we shall see, gained the chief influence among the
Gracchan jurors], and then, through Cicero, the name came to be
used in its final form. *Contra* Wiseman, *Historia* xix (1970) 80
(see ch V, nn. 1f. below).

69 See last note.

70 Free birth would no doubt be demanded; and we may be sure
that good birth, and relation to leading senatorial families, would
continue to count for much. But the basic definition of class
membership would come to be by wealth.

71 Cic. *leg.* iii 20.

72 Varro *ap.* Non. Marc. 728 L.

IV

The Public Companies

1 Frontinus, *aq.* i 7. For some figures for late Republican road repairs see *ILLRP* 464-6: 20 miles of one Apennine highway cost 150,000 sesterces, a Roman street 100 sesterces per foot.

2 *RILR* 81f.

3 E.g. Ürögdi, 1203f.

4 See ch. I, p. 17 above.

5 *ILLRP* 518.

6 This sum is mentioned after the first of the five names (lines 61f.). It is presumably the whole of the contract sum, for which the first man mentioned is *praes*.

7 Festus (as quoted by Paulus: p. 137 L) derives the word from the fact that the *manceps* raised his hand to bid—wrong, but interesting as showing the antiquity of auction practice. He goes on to give a wrong explanation of the phrase 'idem praes', which we in fact find in the Puteoli law. Balsdon (*JRS* lii (1962) 136) is not aware of this evidence, as indeed of most of the evidence concerning public companies.

8 He is *idem praes* (surety as well as buyer), and had to offer *praedia*, which seem to be defined as landed estates situated in Italy. (This seems to be deducible from from Cic. *Fl.* 79f. But it is not at all certain.) There is no point in setting out the various views on the other four men named. (It has even been maintained that they are local magistrates (Kniep, 343)—a counsel of despair, since the local magistrates are in this very document described as *duouiri!*)

9 Pol. vi 17,3 (see Walbank *ad loc.*). Polybius is presumably trying to render the Roman legal terms 'praedes' and 'cognitores', frequently mentioned in connection with public contracts. (E.g. *FIRA* 24, chapters 63-65.) It is not certain who these *cognitores* were; but in effect they were further guarantors for the carrying out of the contract.

10 We have seen the probability of a company's taking part in contracts for both revenues and *ultro tributa*, at least in the time of Cato (see p. 36). On the other side, the great *publicani* (like the father of Plancius: Cic. *Planc.* 32) were prominently involved in many *societates*.

11 Gaius quoted in *dig.* iii 4,1, *pr.*: 'ut ecce uectigalium publicorum sociis permissum est corpus habere, uel aurifodinarum uel argentifodinarum . . .', i.e. apparently all companies of *publicani*. As Kniep points out, it was obviously only the major companies that would take advantage of this permission. Since this grant of

corpus gave the company the right to own property, it should have been possible for the company to offer land as *praedia* when bidding for contracts ; which would have made it practically into a limited-liability company. No such cases are mentioned, and it is generally assumed that it was not possible. Perhaps the grant of *corpus* only followed, in each case, the completion of the letting of the contract, so that the company had no continuing legal existence ; but this would surely have led to difficulties over the vast *familiae* and other properties it owned. There seems, in any case, to be no evidence on this.

12 See pp. 33f. above.

13 Tac. *ann.* xiii 50. Ürögdi is puzzled and takes it as referring to C. Gracchus. But it is difficult to see how the passage can mean that: surely Tacitus did not think that C. Gracchus established companies by law.

14 See *dig.* xvii 2,59, *pr.* ; not with the death of a *socius,* if there was an heir. No special status is mentioned for companies granted *corpus*—indeed, this possibility is not here envisaged. This is only one example of the confused and unsatisfactory nature of our evidence, which makes detailed legal investigation profitless over large areas. The fact that the elder Plancius had been 'plurimarum [societatum] magister' (*Planc.* 32) perhaps suggests that companies existed only for the duration of their particular contract.

15 Livy xliii 16,2.

16 See n. 9 above. In other words, the *adfines* may be *cognitores,* just as the *socii* are *praedes.* But since this latter equation is not necessary, as far as we can tell, the former also may not be.

17 Cic. 2*Verr.* i 143.

18 See ch. II, n. 18.

19 Cic. 2*Verr.* i 133: a new requirement by the inspecting magistrate, added to those of the *lex* for the contract. This was not actually illegal, it seems.

20 Cic. *prov. cons.* 12.

21 See chapter I, pp. 17f. above.

22 E.g. Brunt, 123, 138. As we have already noted, one must not argue from large capital investments or large turnover to large profit margins. Although, as we shall see, in the last age of the Republic profit margins seem to have been enlarged (with the connivance of Roman magistrates) beyond what the *lex censoria* would allow. For the risks of the business, Cic. *l. Man.* 16 gives us good evidence: all the large possessions of the companies would be endangered by war. There is no reason to think they were insured: all we are told is that the contract sum did not have to be paid in case of interference by enemy action. Nor would there be insurance against the sheer panic that Cicero so vividly describes, which might—even without any action to follow—lead

to heavy losses. Moreover, the value of a company's shares (see below) might collapse, for various reasons, just as we can see it going up to new heights in favourable circumstances. Capital invested in a major modern corporation is almost certainly much safer than the capital of the *publicani* was.

23 Cic. *fam.* xiii 10. Brunt (123, n. 9) suggests his losses may be due to the Civil War of 49-8. This can be argued; but I do not believe it. The letter is written early in 46. Cicero writes that young Varro (now Brutus' quaestor), when he first came to the forum (i.e. at age 17 or so), attached himself to Cicero, and then, when fully adult ('ut se corroborauit'), took up two interests close to Cicero's heart: oratory and the *publicani*. He lost heavily in his investments and then 'uersatus in utrisque subselliis' (whatever that means—two kinds of activity in the courts, in any case) he decided, 'iam ante hanc commutationem rei publicae', to become a candidate for office; 'his autem temporibus' he took a letter to Caesar from Cicero when the latter was at Brundisium. Cicero left Brundisium in September 47, after a stay of over ten months (Cic. *fam.* xiv 12 and 20). The *haec commutatio temporum* (taken up by 'his temporibus') is the situation created by Pharsalus. Hence Varro's candidature for office (a military tribunate?) precedes Pharsalus and was probably in 48 (if not 49). If he had time to restore his fortunes by a legal career (sufficiently to stand for office!) before this, he must have spent a few years in the courts. Hence it seems to me quite impossible that his losses were later than (say) 52 or so. More probably Crassus' disaster than the Civil War, in fact; but that was one of the *normal* chances one had to take.

24 See Ürögdi, 1201.

25 Cic. 2*Verr.* ii 172.

26 2*Verr.* iii 166f. (*scribae* 168). All three are quite possibly *equites*: see next note.

27 Verres' own *scriba* is a good example (2*Verr.* iii 185f., implying that the act in itself was quite customary); cf. ibid. 184, showing that, at least in the wider sense of the term, most (if not all) *scribae* claimed to be *equites*. There is no evidence on whether the two *magistri* of the Sicilian company were still active as *scribae* while they held that appointment. If they were, the interlocking of public administration and private enterprise in the public service receives interesting illumination, and further speculation (e.g. on how common this was) is invited. But they may, as *scribae*, have been retired: nothing in Cicero answers the question, or tells us whether *scribae* as such were excluded from the companies. In view of the fact that most restrictions of this kind seem to apply only to senators (so as not to impinge upon the *honestum otium* of the equestrian order), we are perhaps entitled to conclude that *scribae* were not excluded—and that, from the companies' point

of view, they would be very valuable members. But since the matter is uncertain, nothing further may legitimately be built on this. On *scribae* in general, see (not very adequately) Kornemann, *RE*, s.v. 'scriba' (and especially 850f.).

28 *2Verr*. ii 182.

29 *2Verr*. iii 167.

30 *2Verr*. ii 182. For an *a priori* reconstruction of this Sicilian company (not based on Cicero's evidence or any other) see J. P. V. D. Balsdon, *JRS* lii (1962) 135f.

31 *2Verr*. ii 172f. and iii 166 (the same body of men).

32 A pleasant picture is painted by Cicero *2Verr*. ii 31, of the *decumanus* (and it is clear that this is the actual contractor, not only a lowly agent) as 'squaloris plenus ac pulueris'. The Sicilian *decumanus,* owing to the system of the *lex Hieronica,* was evidently quite often (even if Cicero exaggerated) a man in a small way of business, doing his own dirty work.

33 *2Verr*. iii 166 implies that it was by their decision that the records of the *publicani* (i.e. the company) were destroyed. But this, like much in the speech, may be a 'short-hand' rather than a fully technical way of describing the situation. Cf. ii 177 ('decreto *sociorum*'), implying that a regular vote of the general meeting of the company followed.

34 References and discussion Nicolet, 333.

35 *2Verr*. ii 175 'principes et quasi senatores publicanorum'; 'homines honestissimos ac locupletissimos, istos ipsos principes equestris ordinis, quorum splendore . . .'

36 For *ordo publicanorum* see Cic. *Planc*. 23; *fam*. xiii 9,2. In several other cases it might be argued that the *ordo equester* is meant; but in view of the passages cited (where there is no ambiguity) it seems to me preferable to interpret as *ordo publicanorum*: *Q.fr*. i 1,32; 35; *fam*. i 9,26; *Att*. ii 1,8; *l. Man*. 17.

37 Cf. the decrees of the *publicani* on Cicero's exile and recall (*Pis*. 41; *Sest*. 32; *et al*.). When Cicero says 'omnes societates', this obviously implies co-ordination, though presumably separate votes by each company: which would be the most impressive way of managing the vote—like a letter-writing campaign to legislators in the United States.

38 *2Verr*. ii 186f. for the *tabulae* of the company. Carpinatius could not suppress them, so tried to tamper with the entries. He had to let Cicero go over them in detail. For the records, cf. the story of the suppressed correspondence. Even an obstructive governor of outstandingly noble family was afraid of inviting possible prosecution by Cicero by disregarding his legal rights: see *2Verr*. iv 149 (obviously true, at least in outline) for Cicero's successful menaces. The little incident, not often noted, helps to make it certain that Cicero had good connections, which a man like

Metellus had to take seriously. See, for the converse, Plut. *Cic.* 8, *init.*: Cicero's care not to drive the friends of Verres to extremes, and agreeing to a low *litis aestimatio* for Verres. Between them the two passages provide an instructive example of the working of Roman personal politics.

39 *2Verr.* ii 187, 189f.

40 There can be little doubt that the severity of the law that overawed Metellus could have been used to threaten the *publicani*. But Cicero was closely connected with them (*2Verr.* ii 181 shows that he devoted the greater part of his early forensic career to them, no doubt in order to earn their gratitude) and treats this incident with exemplary tact.

41 I.e. men with the powers of a *magister* (cf. 'pro consule' and similar phrases). Our evidence is limited to tax-farming companies, which—in the age of Cicero—are the only ones that matter. We have no evidence on concessions (e.g. mining) or on *ultro tributa* (e.g. military supplies). Presumably, in the case of a large company, the set-up was similar.

42 Thus P. Terentius Hispo—by no means a negligible person, as we shall see—is described as 'qui operas in scriptura pro magistro dat' (*fam.* xiii 65,1). L. Canuleius, 'qui in portu Syracusis operas dabat' (Cic. *2Verr.* ii 171 ; cf. 176), is not actually called *pro magistro* ; but in view of the fact that he writes directly to the company's head office in Rome (ll.cc.: also ibid. 182), just as Carpinatius does, who is called by that title, we may confidently claim him as a holder of that office. Balsdon's imaginary company (*JRS* 1962, 136)—said to be like all companies—has one local *pro magistro* and minor officials. Balsdon is not aware of the fact that 'operas dare' can be applied to the *pro magistro*.

43 *2Verr.* ii 171. The *portus* of Syracuse was part of the *sex publica* of Sicily, on which see ch. III, n. 55.

44 Both together *2Verr.* ii 170f. Canuleius bears the name of a plebeian family of early distinction. But it is unlikely that he was directly connected with that family ; the name is not uncommon. The name 'Carpinatius', on the other hand, is very rare: it never appears elsewhere in the literary sources and only once in the whole of *CIL* (vi 14 414).

45 Cicero never uses that word of any person a Roman senator or knight ought to know: it positively implies ignorance of the person concerned, in the best circles.

46 Cic. *fam.* xiii 65,1f.

47 Cic. *Att.* xi 10,1. Perhaps he retired as a result of the civil war and Caesar's activities in the East.

48 Münzer, *RE*, s.v. 'Terentius', no. 49. (Though he is mistaken in suggesting relationship to Cicero's wife: see Shackleton Bailey's note on *Att.*, l.c.—indeed, such relationship, constituting actual

adfinitas with Cicero himself, ought to have been mentioned in the letter recommending the man.) Cicero's friend Ser. Sulpicius, *cos.* 51, was son of a Quintus and may well be related to Hispo's wife ; though not closely (e.g. her brother), since otherwise (again) Cicero ought to have mentioned it in a letter written in 51.

49 In view of our extreme dearth of information, it would be interesting to know the exact status of P. Cuspius. Cicero (*fam.* xiii 6-6a) clearly made special efforts to oblige this man, but gives us no very precise details, since his correspondent seems to have known who the man was. Cicero merely says that he had been in Africa twice while in charge of the most important affairs of a public company. This may mean that he had had two spells as *pro magistro*. However, it may also mean (and I take this as more probable) that he had twice, as *magister* of a company with African interests, visited that province on specially important business. We cannot reasonably conjecture what that business might be.

50 Frequently in Cicero, e.g. *Att.* v 15, *fin.* ; 16, *init.*

51 2*Verr.* iii 165f. Calderone, *Kokalos* x-xi, 1964-65, 76f. appears to use this arrangement in support of his fanciful thesis regarding the *sex publica*. (See ch. III, n. 55). In fact, of course, it has nothing to do with the precise scope of the company's activities. It is merely due to its size and importance.

52 2*Verr.* iii 168.

53 Ibid. 167.

54 See especially Catullus' curses for a less obliging governor: Cat. 10 and 28. On Cicero's own experience, see *Att.* vii 1,6.

55 Ibid., with *fam.* ii 17,4. The million sesterces (it is fair to add) was left after a year's estimated expenses had been set aside for the quaestor who was to take over from him (this, no doubt—though we are not told, since it is taken for granted—was left in a separate account with the *publicani*). It is not certain what Cicero did with the proceeds of the sale of the prisoners of war whom he had captured and sold (*Att.* v 20,5: the sum itself is quite uncertain, though the figure suggested by Shackleton Bailey *ad loc.* seems the most reasonable: 120,000 HS). In his letter telling Atticus of his arrangements about leaving the surplus (see last note) he says that the surplus is out of his annual allowance. In the letter mentioning his plan to leave it in the province (*fam., cit.*) he says that no one shall touch his booty 'except the city quaestors'. If this is to be taken literally, he was planning to take it to Rome— which is incredible, since the arguments he gives to Atticus against transporting money by sea would still apply. Perhaps that sum is to be added to what he left in the province out of his allowance. (But, if so, it is odd that he does not mention it to Atticus.) All his references to his surplus are vague and seem a little shifty. See next note.

56 On his lawful (as he insists) profit, see *Att.* xi 1,2 (cf. 2,1) ; *fam.* v 20,9. (It is not at all clear what happened to this money ; but it looks as though Cicero was not entirely candid about the whole business.)

57 Cic. *Pis.* 86 (18 million sesterces). If this is true (it is by no means incredible), this must be because for some reason he could not imitate Verres' course: investment by the governor in his own province—where he could charge what he liked and make sure it was paid—would obviously have been more profitable. Piso (we must admit) was not on good terms with the *publicani* ; but it may also be that the Macedonian *societates* could not handle the large sums involved.

58 Cic. *2Verr.* iii 20.

59 Ibid. 25f.—explicitly asserted to apply to all provinces (27). Verres' reversal of this (despite modern attempts at whitewash) deserves all the execration it receives here.

60 Ibid. 44 ('nihil istius simile facturum').

61 Cic. *Att.* v 13,1. In the next letter (14,1) he seems to have found two equally pleasing items of news: that the Parthians were not attacking, and that his predecessor had managed to quell an army mutiny. This sheds light on the importance of the *pactiones*.

62 Cic. *Att.* v 13,1.

63 Cic. *fam.* xiii 65,1.

64 See the latter cited last note ; and, e.g., xiii 6,4.

65 *2Verr.* iii 28f.

66 *Q.fr.* i 1: 60 B.C. (The citations from sections 32-35.) On Quintus' own ambitions, to be discerned as early as this, see Wiseman, *JRS* lvi (1966) 110.

67 *2Verr.* iii 181-4. Cicero's indignation makes it difficult to see how much of this was done elsewhere. We can only guess. The exchange fee (*collybus*) seems to have been collected elsewhere, since Cicero is indignant at it only because Sicily has a uniform currency. The fee of 4 per cent for the *scriba* was clearly common enough, and helped to account for the wealth and standing of that class. (Cf. n. 27 above). These, of course, were the governor's exactions ; but it is only too likely that the *publicani* would feel encouraged to imitate the example he set. One additional imposition by Verres is roundly denounced as illegal, and we must accept this: a cash charge for knocking down the tithe at the time of the auction. This, obviously, had to be passed on to the customer. The story illustrates the essential soundness of C. Gracchus' system of *censoria locatio*.

68 For fees charged by the governor, which may (where appropriate) have been passed on and would in any case invite imitation, see last note. A one per cent 'collection fee' is attested *Rab. Post.* 30. (See also the 'approval fee' *2Verr.* iii 73.) We do not know whether

the *lex censoria* had by then taken official notice of it or whether it was one of those points in which it was wiser not to insist on one's rights. The way in which a governor could, by seemingly legal and specious means, exert intolerable pressure is again indicated by Verres' edicts. (See 2*Verr*. iii 35f.—showing clearly *why* it might be wiser, even for an *eques Romanus* in the province, not to insist on his rights!) Exactions beyond what was due go back a long way—perhaps to the days before *publicani* collected the tax. Cicero's reference to the good old days when the natives used to heap up the wheat in the measures beyond the legal level, out of pure good will for a fair collector (2*Verr*. iii 118), may in fact recall a time (in the second century) when this 'voluntary' and informal contribution was the only extra-legal exaction.

69 2*Verr*. ii 186—not to mention the rapacity of Apronius and others, to whom he sold the taxes, sharing in their profits. Carpinatius is alleged by Cicero to have been in league with Verres ; but it must be assumed that much of the profit he made was the company's. It is clear from their reaction to Verres' initial attempt to cheat them that the *magistri* of the company were shrewd businessmen, not easily taken in. Their decision, not only to honour Verres, but to take the risk of suppressing evidence against him, must have had a firmer basis in facts and figures than a laudatory letter or two from Carpinatius. We must again note how astutely Cicero avoids any offence to the *publicani* of Rome, for political reasons. In this case, the *pro magistro* has to be painted as a lone villain.

70 Brunt, 125, n. 2, points to the *lex Antonia de Termessibus* (*FIRA* 11), *ad fin*. He claims that the terms are 'not quite appropriate to an inland city' and that they must 'represent a standard form'. He gives no reason for this opinion or the conclusion drawn from it. The last sentence (fragmentary) gives reason to believe that the immunity from local *portoria* given to Roman *publicani* applied to them only in the exercise of their 'official' functions. Indeed, in that capacity a large company would have to move large quantities of goods of various kinds, in addition to the tribute grain itself. The clause provides no evidence for trading activities.

71 See Cic. *Att*. ii 16,4f.

V

Equites, Senators, Armies

1 Some suggestions in Brunt, 141f.

2 We do not know for certain which had been set up by the time of Sulla ; but some may be safely conjectured, and at least one (the *maiestas* court) is known. See *Historia* xi (1962) 207f. (I should now put the degrees of probability rather differently.)

3 See *MRR* i 537 (Vestals) ; 546 (Mamilius) ; Gruen, 127f. ; 140f.

4 The fact that this could happen, without radically affecting the land-owning economic basis of the equestrian class as a whole, is briefly and brilliantly brought out by Brunt.

5 Pliny's principal statement is quoted ch. III, n. 68, with brief discussion.

6 *MRR* ii 126f. On the importance of the year 70, I have had something to say in my Todd Lecture, *Lucius Sulla* (1970), in a re-evaluation after U. Laffi's discussion, *Athenaeum* lv (1967) 113f. ; 255f.

7 We happen to have this securely attested in a famous anecdote about Pompey (Plut. *Pomp.* 22).

8 See Nicolet, 190f.

9 *MRR* ii 145. I am not convinced by Wiseman's argument on the other side (*Historia* xix (1970) 72) from the putative number of seats in a modern restoration of the Theatre of Pompey ; nor from the fixed number of rows in the *lex Roscia*: one might argue in the same way from the seating arrangements in the House of Commons. We do not know how many rows were reserved for *equites* (in the strict sense) before they lost the privilege ; but in any case, Roman legal thinking would favour a fixed number (cf. the insistence on *certa pecunia*). And in ancient economic conditions, a fair amount of stability could be assumed in whatever the numbers were at the time. (Provincial *equites* would hardly have to be considered.) Nor can I agree with the view of Cicero as a purist and reactionary in the use of the term 'equites'. (In this, Wiseman himself (n. 74) has to admit confusion ; but it is simpler to avoid it.) See also next note. But the article provides an excellent summary of the complex sources.

10 Cic. *Mur.* 40—proclaiming general gratification in extravagant terms. If (as Wiseman suggests—see last note) Cicero was being reactionary and praising a law that conferred this dignity only on *equites* in the strict sense, keeping out those who were calling themselves by that title (and who would obviously be annoyed at being kept out!), then Cicero, as a lawyer, should have had more sense than to please one third of his jury at the price of

deeply wounding another third (the *tribuni aerarii*—according to Wiseman, precisely those against whom the law was directed). This offends against all the rhetorical principles he constantly practises and preaches. For the dissatisfaction of the plebs, see Plut. *Cic.* 13. (That much of the anecdote, no doubt, may be believed: cf. Pliny, *n.h.* vii 117; and it throws an interesting light on Cicero's assertion of popular favour for the law (*Mur.* l.c.; Asc. 78f.).)

11 This is Wiseman's suggestion (*op. cit.*): he plausibly argues that the title may have been an antiquarian revival, since the real *tribuni aerarii* were no longer needed after 167 B.C. Possibly, however, they had led a nominal life ever since: Roman institutions clung to life with tough conservatism. In any case, it is clear from our evidence (see Wiseman's collection of sources) that they could be called *equites* by Cicero when it suited him.

12 This has often been noted, especially in recent years. It is well formulated by Gruen (124): 'One cannot regard the equestrian class as a closed bloc, likely to vote as a unit on all issues.' (He goes on, however, to say that 'interference with business interests in the provinces could arouse united hostility'. I cannot see any reason for this supposed exception.)

13 All *domi nobiles,* at least in major towns, must have been *equites* in the wider sense (though not, as Nicolet rightly insists, in the strict sense of having been placed on the censors' lists of *equites*). Many of these, of course, will have had shares in business enterprises, especially the public companies; but they were basically landed squires. Life in those circles was not always idyllic: the events recounted in Cicero's *pro Cluentio* have a Compton-Burnett flavour.

14 Pliny, *n.h.* xxxiii 34. This was Hill's justification for describing them as a 'middle class' (see his Preface to *The Roman Middle Class* (1952)).

15 *MRR* i 553. Marius had promised to finish the war quickly if elected. But 107 and most of 106 passed with no essential change in the situation. (The battles of Sall. *Jug.* 97f. come only at the end of the year, when Marius is moving into winter quarters.)

16 Cic. *de or.* i 225; cf. *Br.* 164. (Note 'Eripite ex faucibus eorum quorum crudelitas nostro sanguine non potest expleri; nolite sinere nos cuiquam seruire nisi uobis [i.e. the People] uniuersis, quibus et possumus et debemus.') For the rhetorical habit of describing exile in terms of bloody massacre, see E. Wistrand, *Sallust and Judicial Murders in Rome* (1968).

17 See Gruen's discussion, especially ch. VI.

18 Cic. *Br.* 128 (whatever the phrase 'Gracchani iudices' means). See the useful discussion Gruen, 159.

19 See Earl, *Latomus* xxiv (1965) 532f.

20 See my study *Historia* xviii (1969) 447f. The ordinary citizen, at least by the age of Cicero, had no love for the tax-collector, i.e. especially the *portitor*: see Cic. *Q.fr.* i 1,33 for their *iniuriae* even in Italy.

21 See the interesting and challenging reflections on wealth at Rome —supported by all the information I am aware of—in Wiseman, *Historia* xix (1970) 76f. (*Contra* Meier, 66f., with little concrete evidence.) Men of equestrian wealth, again—however low they might seem to a senator—were few in number and an élite. Wiseman conjectures that those of mere equestrian wealth, who liked to call themselves '*equites*', were comparatively few, in proportion to those enrolled by the censors in that class. On Glaucia's law restoring the courts (104, 101 or 100) see Greenidge-Clay[2], 100f.

22 Q. Mucius Scaevola the Augur (not to be confused with his cousin the Pontifex, on whom see below): *MRR* i 523f. Cf. C. Cichorius, *Unters. zu Lucilius* (1908), 237f.

23 C. Cato. See Gruen, 127. All the known cases are enumerated in his Appendix E (pp. 305-8). Meier (70f., especially 77f.), at his best in the sensitive appreciation of the Roman social structure, writes (perhaps) his very best pages on this period in general.

24 See notes 22 and 23. The only possible evidence of political justice is the special tribunal that sentenced Q. Caepio, the consul who had passed the law removing the jury courts from complete equestrian control. On this, see Gruen, 162f. He was convicted of having stolen the gold captured at Tolosa, and may well have been guilty. (Gruen says that the charge of embezzlement 'is strongly implied, though not explicitly stated'. His quotation from Orosius in n. 29 omits the explicit statement in that author: 'Caepio . . . cuncta per scelus furatus fuisse narratur'.)

25 Cf. the case of M' Aquillius, around 95 B.C. (Sources Greenidge-Clay[2], 116.)

26 Cic. 1*Verr.* 38.

27 Diod. xxxvi 3, *init.* Cf. *RILR* 54.

28 Cic. *Att.* v 21,10f.; vi 1,4f.; 2,7f.; 3,5f. Cf. *RILR* 82f.

29 Ptolemy Alexander I—see *RM* cx (1967) 178f. We do not know what security Ariobarzanes of Cappadocia had given. The Senate decree (Diod. l.c.) does not specify *illegal* enslavement.

30 Rostovtzeff, *SEHHW* ii 782, puzzled by their organizing slave raids themselves, imagines that they bought slaves kidnapped by tribesmen! Yet in the very same context he realizes that Nicomedes regarded his subjects (not in cities) as his property and had no hesitation in enslaving them for debt or any other worthy cause; in fact, he says that Nicomedes (on evidence from Delphi and unconnected with this incident) 'was certainly an active slave dealer'. It is surprising that prejudice against the *publicani* (whom he regards, on this evidence alone—there is no other—as organizing

the slave trade) has blinded him to the truth he almost stumbled on. (There is, of course, no doubt that the *publicani* were money-lenders: they had to invest the large sums they collected.) According to a well-known passage in Strabo (xiv 5,2), the main market at Delos could sell tens of thousands of slaves a day—obviously not all physically present on the island at the same time! This shows the sophisticated international organization of the slave trade (not to be ascribed to Cilician pirates). It is unlikely that the *publicani* practised it as a side-line, without our hearing of it. Though, of course, some of the same individuals may easily have been involved in both lines of business.

31 In fact, Diodorus goes on to relate how the Senate's precipitate reaction indirectly led to the great slave war in Sicily. The shock was obviously genuine. This story is one of several reasons for not taking Cicero's rhetorical point (2*Verr.* iii 94f.) too seriously.

32 *RILR,* especially ch. VI.

33 On the mission of Scaevola, see *Athenaeum* xliv (1956) 120f.; *Studies* 170f. On Rutilius, see *RE,* s.v. 'Rutilius', no. 34: he was born not later than 158. The trouble in Asia was probably due to lack of proper supervision of both Romans and native magistrates.

34 On *dioeceses,* see Magie, *Roman Rule in Asia Minor* (1950) i 171f.; II 1059f. (notes 41-44). The system was not a continuation of Hellenistic arrangements, and we first pick it up for certain after Sulla. In view of what we know of Scaevola's reorganization, he is probably the most obvious candidate for its foundation. Sicily, under the *lex Hieronica* (as adapted by Rome), may have provided the example. In spite of what is sometimes asserted or implied, there is no clear evidence that the system of *conuentus* (the Latin term for *dioeceses*) was in operation in any non-Greek province even in the age of Cicero.—It is possible that Scaevola also had something to do with the founding (or at least the Roman recognition) of the Asian provincial meeting (*koinon* or *commune*); see Magie, *op. cit.* i 174 (with notes), and cf. J. Deininger, *Die Provinziallandtage* (1965), 14f. For his recognition of Greek judges (and therefore Greek law), later followed by Cicero in Cilicia, see Cic. *Att.* vi 1,15. (I take this to be the meaning of the words. See Shackleton Bailey *ad loc.*)

35 See *RILR* 29 (with notes). Ptolemy Apion died in 96.

36 It was in 94 that the Senate passed a decree somehow limiting moneylending to provincials. We have no details, since we hear of it only incidentally in a much later context (Asc. 57). But it must surely be connected with the events we have noted around this time. On action, about this time, to improve the state of Sicily, see Diod. xxxvii 8.

37 See Gruen, 308, under 97 and 95 B.C.

38 Cic. *fam.* i 9,26.

39 *Why* he was not attacked is more of a puzzle than scholars care to admit. I suggested (*Studies* 44, 58) that Marius, recently become an *adfinis* of his cousin, saved him, and I still think this as good an answer as any. Scaevola (unlike most senior nobles) did not fight against Marius and Cinna in 87 and escaped their vengeance, remaining in Rome to give authority to Cinna's régime.

40 Asc. 15 (with my comments *Athenaeum* 1956, 106). Balsdon, *CR* li (1937) 8f. is in error.

41 For the sources on the trial see Greenidge-Clay², 125f. Marius' part in the affair is made clear by Dio xxviii 97,3. Rutilius had been Metellus' legate in Africa and had remained loyal to him—unlike Marius, who had used his similar position to intrigue against him; as consul 105, Rutilius claimed credit (with some justice, as far as we can see) for building the 'new model army' that Marius later led against the Germans (Val. Max. ii 3,2, with Front. *str.* iv 2,2). Festus 316-7, s.v. 'Rufuli', helps to confirm this.

42 Note his *lex de prouinciis consularibus* (Greenidge-Clay² 37f.; cf. ch. III, n. 37).

43 Cic. *ap.* Asc. 21.

44 Asc. l.c. See *Athenaeum* 1956, 120f.; Gruen, 206 (adding further details).

45 M. Drusus cannot be discussed in detail. Sources Greenidge-Clay², 128f. See my discussions *For. Cl.* 215f., *Studies* 40f., for my views. His main authoritative sponsors were M. Scaurus and L. Crassus.

46 Crassus was the author (with Scaevola) of the law of 95 that pushed many Italians into despair (see *Historia* 1969, 489) and his censorship in 92 made the problem seem acute for them. For M. Scaurus' attitude, see his famous remark, said to have been one of the main causes of that harsh law (see Cic. *de or.* ii 257, explained by P. Fraccaro, *Opuscula* ii (1957) 132f.). Gruen refuses to admit that politicians can change their minds ('Crassus was the last man to defend a policy of enfranchisement' (212)—for no visible reason except that he had opposed it earlier); he supports this by the misstatement that in 92, as censors, Crassus and his colleague had issued an edict expelling Latin teachers of rhetoric (203—for the facts, see *Historia* 1969, 488f.: there was no expulsion). Crassus' attitude in 91 is clear from his 'swan song' in the Senate, defending the Senate (which had supported Drusus' plans, *including* the proposal for enfranchisement) against attack by the hostile consul L. Philippus. (The incident is cited by Gruen, who tries to explain it away.) Chr. Meier (212) calls Cicero's view that Drusus attempted to reaffirm senatorial control of the state, and that his legislation on the allies was part of this plan, 'durchaus unwahrscheinlich', alleging that the Senate's position was not so bad that this should have been necessary. I hope I have shown that Cicero and our other sources

make it clear that their version is essentially correct. Meier proposes an alternative: perhaps the attempt to 'split' the *equites* was a necessary preliminary for securing the citizenship for Italians! To support this, he has to make up an elaborate story of opposition by the *equites* to Italian enfranchisement, totally unattested in the sources. Irresponsible rejection of well-supported sources often leads to the writing of historical fiction.

47 Brunt (120f.) seems to me to put this in precisely the right perspective. (But his list (n. 3) of *noui homines* just before 100 B.C. is inaccurate: remove Cn. Aufidius ; add, at least, T. Albucius, C. Coelius Caldus (one of the most important, rising to the consulship), and Vibius (*MRR* i 563).)

48 The panel of the *lex Acilia* had provided for 450 jurors (*FIRA* 7, 12f.) ; and since then several standing courts had been added, and—as Sulla later saw—more were needed. The Senate, at this time, had about 300 members. On Senate debates, see *RE,* s.v. 'Senatus', *Suppl.* vi, coll. 705f.: no one of quaestorian rank is ever recorded as having spoken, and it is unlikely that anyone ever did. (Cato, in the Catilinarian debate, spoke as tribune elect. In any case, he was unique.) Even ex-tribunes would not normally have a chance.

49 Cic. *Cluent.* 153.

50 For Titinius, see *RE,* s.v. ; Maecenas, Sall. *hist.* iii 83M. (A twenty-year interval does not as such preclude identity.)

51 See ch. IV, n. 27.

52 Cic. l.c. (n. 49) ; cf. *Rab. Post.* 16. Of course, there were *some* ambitious men (see Brunt, 120, perhaps slightly exaggerating): there had always been some, and some had always secured advancement.

53 Cic. *de or.* iii, *init.*

54 I have discussed this in detail in *Historia* 1969, 447f.

55 Cic. *Rosc. Am.* 140. Accepted Meier, 219 (with reservations), chiefly for the odd reason that 'what we hear about the circle of those proscribed by Sulla fully confirms this evidence'. It might be pertinent to ask whether the 'evidence' was not invented in order to justify what happened in the proscriptions. See *Studies,* 206f., especially 222f.

56 See, e.g., Cic. *2Verr.* i 35 (misinterpreted Meier, 219). Cf. *Studies, cit.*

57 Gabba, *ASNP,* s.2, xxxiii (1964) 1f.

58 See my Todd Lecture, *Lucius Sulla* (1970).

59 1,600 *equites* are said to have been proscribed (App. *b.c.* i 95,442 ; Flor. ii 9,25 implies a higher number). Their wealth may have had almost as much to do with it as their political activities, as many stories in the sources suggest. Sulla's *odium in equestrem ordinem* (Cic. *Cluent.* 151) is introduced for forensic reasons and belied

by Sulla's settlement; but the fact is that *equites* (like Jews, at times, in more recent periods of history) were both wealthy and helpless. It paid to call some of them enemies.

60 It has occasionally been suggested by modern scholars (e.g. Hill, 147, with references); but hardly the enriched centurion Fufidius (Sall. *hist.* i 55, 22 M)!

61 This is discussed n. 9 above and text.

62 See Brunt, *Latomus* xv (1956) 17f.: there is no solid evidence for such a view. To be fair, there is none for the retention of the system either. But in the case of a sweeping and short-lived reform, about the reversal of which we hear nothing, the onus of proof is on those who would assert it.

63 Cic. *2Verr.* iii 18. (Correct the date in Brunt, 124, n. 8.)

64 See ch. III, nn. 40f. and text.

65 See Sherk, *RDGE,* no. 23.

66 Sall. *hist.* ii 43 M. Cf. *RILR* 35f.

67 See my Todd Lecture *Lucius Sulla* (1970).

68 See n. 6 above. Sources on the *lex Aurelia MRR* ii 127. On *tribuni aerarii* see n. 11 above.

69 Cic. *Mur.* 69.

70 Cic. *2Verr.* iii 168: 'certe huic homini spes nulla salutis esset si publicani, hoc est si equites Romani, iudicarent.' This does not mean (as is often stated) that Cicero identified *equites* and *publicani,* as might appear when the phrase 'publicani, hoc est . . . equites Romani' is quoted in this form out of its context. (Thus, e.g., *RE, Suppl.* xi, 1196.)

71 This was shown long ago by E. Gabba, *Le origini della guerra sociale e la vita politica romana dopo l'89 a.C.* (1954). (That part of his thesis remains intact.) Meier, 66f., gives an excellent brief account of the interconnection between the two parts of the equestrian class.

72 Cic. *l. Man.* 17f.

73 Cic. *Planc.* 23f., 32f.

74 See ch. III, nn. 1f. and text.

75 Val. Max. vi 9,7.

76 See Sherk, *RDGE,* no. 4, l.18 (*c.* 160 B.C.): a T. Aufidius as witness to a Senate decree; Cn. Aufidius T.f. (*SIG*[3] 715 (late second century B.C.)) is probably his son.

77 Cic. *Pis.* 41 'equites Romanos in prouincia, . . . publicanos nobiscum et uoluntate et dignitate coniunctos'.

78 Cic. *Planc.* 23. He often repeats the general sentiment.

79 Though not all, like C. Curtius in Cicero's youth (*Rab. Post.* 3), can be said even by Cicero to have sought wealth only to do good.

80 Brunt (121) rightly shows that voting on juries (where we have figures) does not reveal the panels delivering bloc votes.

81 Brunt (148f.) rightly draws attention to this.

82 Plut. *Luc*. 20.

83 See *RILR,* ch. VI.

84 Documented Brunt, l.c. I cannot believe that it was only honest dislike of a command successfully held for over four years (with some of the greatest victories in Roman history) that was responsible for withdrawing Asia from his sphere precisely in 69 (see *MRR* ii 133), at the first opportunity after his Asian settlement.

85 Cic. 2*Verr*. iii 12. Strictly speaking, he gives no positive information on Sardinia, Macedonia, Gaul, and Cyrene, except that we may infer their system was not like the Sicilian one. Cyrene, when reorganized in 75/4, may conceivably have had *censoria locatio* introduced. For the others it is rather unlikely: in Gaul we could have expected to hear of it, e.g. in the *pro Fonteio* ; in the case of the other two, it would have involved an act of positive reorganization—and if for Macedonia or Sardinia, why not for Africa, which was far more lucrative? (On Macedonia, see also n. 89 and text.)

86 See *RILR* 75.

87 Cic. *fam*. xiii 9.

88 Cic. *prov. cons*. 10.

89 Cic. *Pis*. 87.

90 *MRR* ii 187f., 190 (Vatinius).

91 Cic. *Att*. i 17,9. We do not know who the censors were, but Dio xxxvii 46,4, confirms that there were censors: they enlarged the Senate by generosity in adlection. There was no *lustrum*. The most recent discussion (Balsdon, *JRS* 1962, 136) shows strange unawareness of the historical and economic background, but rightly rejects *Schol. Bob*. 157f. as a mere guess.

92 Cic. l.c. This, at least, was the amount Caesar later conceded (Dio xxxviii 7,4 ; App. *b.c.* ii 13 ; Suet. *Jul*. 20, with a fatherly warning). Balsdon (*JRS* 1962, 136f.) asks why the companies unsuccessful in 61 did not protest, but finds no answer. There is an obvious one: they could now find all the business they wanted in Pompey's new provinces!

93 Cic. *Q.fr*. i 1,32f. (Note 'hic te ita uersari ut et publicanis satisfacias, praesertim publicis male redemptis, ac socios perire non sinas, diuinae cuiusdam uirtutis esse uidetur'—it is perhaps not surprising that Quintus never rose to the consulship.) Cf. *Att*. 1 17,9f. (Note 'ut illi auderent hoc postulare, Crassus eos impulit.')

94 Cic. 2*Verr*. iii 130, 140 *et al*.

95 Decimus Brutus (*cos*. 77): Cic. 2*Verr*. i 144, 150.

96 Ch. I, n. 16. The only one added later (as far as we know) was the temple of Mars Ultor (Dio lv 10,5): clearly to give it special prestige.

97 For the petition, see above: M. Crassus does not appear as a *socius*. For Gabinius, see *Q.fr.* ii 13,2.

98 Cic. *Vat.* 29 ; cf. Pocock's edition, App. IV c, arguing from this that Vatinius must have been actively involved in passing the laws of Caesar.

99 *Staatspacht* 372f. For the fourth ('particula'), see n. 101 ; there the origin is even less reliable. The statement is taken over by Ürögdi.

100 Cic. *Rab. Post.* 4.

101 Val. Max. vi 9,7. (This must be the origin of Rostovtzeff's 'Stock Exchange jargon' term 'particula'—needless to say, Valerius probably made it up.) If Aufidius had not been registered as a *socius,* the fact that he was one would presumably not have been common knowledge, to be held against him later. Unregistered investment, by this time, was not dishonourable, if Caesar could openly practise it.

102 Cic. *Vat.* 13, 15, *et al.*

103 See n. 93. Nor even (we may add) merely in order to stir up political trouble: as I have shown in other cases (*RILR,* ch. VI), personal, political, and economic motives become inseparably intertwined in the late Republic.

104 This is not to deny that an odd senator might even then have an interest in a company through a freedman—precisely as the elder Cato had in trade (Plut. *Cat. Mai.* 21). But presumably this would (like Cato's action) be rare and frowned upon ; and it is noteworthy that Cato (as we have seen) does not even consider *publica* as a source of income (*agr., praef.*). We must not think in terms of fantastic profits before C. Gracchus.

105 Again we find all kinds of interests thoroughly intertwined. Cic. *fam.* xiii 9, stressing his close ties with the Bithynian company, may be significant. Note also, e.g., the tactful wording in such passages as *fam.* xiii 65,2: 'ex huius obseruantia gratissimi hominis et ex sociorum gratia hominum amplissimorum maximum fructum capies.'

106 See *RILR* 80f.

107 Relevant figures are given in Plut. *Pomp.* 45, from Pompey's own tabulation. It might be held that it was, on the whole, to the advantage of the provincials if there was not an abnormal amount of competition for tax contracts in Rome. Whatever the theoretical position, it is amply clear from the evidence we have surveyed that an excessively high bid by the company would in fact mean excessively high burdens to be passed on to the provincials.

108 Dio xxxvii 51,3 (confused in detail) ; Cic. *Att.* ii 16,2. It was no doubt an attempt to gain popularity for himself, probably (as Carcopino suggested) backed by Pompey (cf. Cic. l.c.: Pom-

pey seems to have gloried in the fact that his new *uectigalia,* acquired overseas, would suffice to support the state). In 63/2, Metellus had been a staunch adherent of Pompey (see *MRR* ii 174: he even fled to Pompey from Rome, thus providing him— had he wanted it, as Caesar later did—with a pretext for armed intervention). In 60, although his brother Celer, as consul, led the opposition to Pompey (Dio xxxvii 49,3f.: he acted out of resentment at Pompey's divorce of his cousin or sister Mucia), Nepos is not mentioned in this connection and probably preferred not to forfeit Pompey's friendship, at least until he had his consulate. Dio xxxvii 51,3 implies that his own brother opposed this law; which both shows that the two brothers were not necessarily pursuing the same line at the time and suggests that Pompey may have had an interest in the law. These tariffs had been very unpopular (Cic. *Q.fr.* i 1,33), and their abolition was presumably the small price that Pompey (for the sake of his political standing) exacted from the *publicani* in return for their vastly increased business. They were henceforth not likely to be short of investment opportunities.

109 The delay, as we saw, was very unfortunate for the taxpayers in the province.

110 See Cic. *Vat.* (n. 98 and text).

111 Cic. *Att.* v 15,3. (On *dioeceses* in general, see n. 34 above).

112 On this reorganization, see Syme, *Buckler Studies* (1939), 301f. for 'nostrarum dioecesium' in this sense, see *Att.* v 21,7. But Cilicia also had *dioeceses* (*Att.* vi 2,4).

113 *Att.* v 16,1.

114 It is interesting that only the *scriptura* and *portorium* of the *dioeceses* are mentioned (v 15,3). We can only speculate about the reasons for this limitation, which must (in any case) be deliberate. It may be a very simple one, e.g. that *scriptura* and *portorium* necessitated a much more frequent exchange of correspondence with Rome (cf. the information we get from the *Verrines*) than the *decuma,* which, for parts of the year, must have been a fairly quiet line of business. In any case, Cicero's concern here is with the speed and frequency of the postal service.

115 Cic. *fam.* xiii 9,2: 'constat enim ex ceteris societatibus'. I do not see how the Latin can be taken in any other sense whatever: there is not a clearer sentence in the whole of Cicero. We must explain it as we find it.

116 Cic. *Fl.* 11 ; cf. *2Verr.* iii 94 (clearly untrue as far as *equites* as a whole were concerned, but probably applicable to *publicani*).

117 This seems to be what Fonteius did in Gaul (Cic. *Font.* 19f. (unfortunately incomplete)), quite apart from some shady dealings over road contracts, which recall Verres (ibid. 17f.).

118 Verres had sold censorships in the cities and let the censors re-

imburse themselves at the expense of the citizens (*2Verr.* ii 131f., especially 138). Appius in Cilicia had let the rich in the cities get away with every sort of peculation and oppression of their fellow-citizens (Cic. *Att.* vi 2,5 ; cf. ibid. 1,2).

119 *MRR* ii 247. The career of C. Verres might well have been similar, had he not been unlucky in his prosecutor.

120 Ch. IV, n. 57 and text.

121 Cic. *prov. cons.* 5.

122 Cic. *Pis.* 87.

123 Cic. *prov. cons.* and *Pis., passim.*

124 *MRR* ii 203. The refusal shows powerful interests working against him in Rome.

125 *MRR* ii 218.

126 See *MRR,* l.c.

127 See my Todd Lecture *Lucius Sulla.* On the numbers of senators, see Gabba's discussion in his *Appiani Bellorum Ciuilium Liber Primus,* pp. 343f. The figures for senators killed are variously given and unreliable in detail. But the facts that the Senate before Sulla had a paper strength of 300 (App. *b.c.* i 35, 158 (with Gabba's note) ; Plut. *C. Gr.* 5 ; Livy, *per.* lx) and later of 600 (Gabba, l.c., with references) ; that the last census had been in 86, so that a loss of (perhaps) fifty members must be expected by natural wastage ; and that murders (App. *b.c.* i 88, 403), proscriptions (ib. 95, 442) and fighting had undoubtedly inflicted heavy losses on the senatorial order as on others—these facts make it clear that far more than 300 *equites* (thus Appian, *b.c.* i 100, 468) must have been added, even if (as Gabba rightly observes) those men of senatorial family with any shadow of a claim would get preference. Appian's figure is probably not to be taken very seriously: it could easily be arrived at by simply subtracting the pre-Sullan figure of 300 senators from the post-Sullan figure of 600, and I suspect Appian's source may have had no better evidence than that.

128 See Cic. *Cluent.* 153 ; and cf. n. 49 and text (above). Though it must be admitted that the elder Plancius, on one occasion, acted like a survivor of that generation (*Planc.* 33f.).

129 The elder Plancius supports his son's candidature, and Cicero implies that this is common (*Planc.* 24). L. Aelius Lamia (*RE,* s.v. 'Aelius', no. 75) and C. Rabirius Postumus (*RE,* s.v. 'Rabirius', no. 6) entered the Senate. Cicero's friend Atticus was exceptional in many ways. Though, of course, we must continue to assume that the vast majority of the 'businessmen' *equites* had no political ambitions, either for themselves or for their families—as, indeed, is the case in all societies and all ages. (See n. 157 below.)

130 See *RILR* 62f.

131 Chief sources Cic. *Att.* i 17,9 ; *Planc.* 34f., with *Schol. Bob.* 157f.
(St.). The scholiast professes detailed information, not all of
which seems reliable: he is given to embroidering what he can
gather from his actual text. (That there had been a *hostilis
incursio* in Asia in 61, which was the reason for the request, is
not mentioned by Cicero, who could hardly have failed to
mention it ; all the more so since his brother was governor at
the time!) For a bad case of this, see p. 129 (St.), on the *lex
Licinia Mucia*.

132 *Sest.* 21 ; cf. *Planc.* 50: a noble who makes a real effort is never
turned down.

133 For the facts see Sall. *Cat.* 52f. Cato's moral excellence (stressed
by Sallust) may be granted, for the sake of argument. The fact,
nevertheless, is without precedent.

134 L. Aelius Lamia (n. 129 above).

135 See ch. IV, n. 37.

136 See *RILR,* ch. VI.

137 On Gabinius see p. 109 (above): it was the *repetundae* charge
that succeeded. A discussion over Gabinius in the Senate brought
about a clash between the representatives of the *publicani* and
the offensive noble L. Domitius (Cic. *Q.fr.* ii 13,2).

138 Cic. *Q.fr.* i 1.

139 *RE,* s.v. 'Sergius', no. 23 ; *MRR* ii 155.

140 On Appius see the sources collected *MRR* ii 229 (especially Cic.
Att. v 16,2 ; vi 1,2). It has become fashionable to disbelieve
Cicero, without evidence to the contrary. There is no reason for
doubting the facts he gives. On Lentulus, see *MRR* ii 210, 218.
(Cf. next note.)

141 Cic. *Att.* v 21,7—and that (as I pointed out *RILR* 87) just after
Cato had carried off 7,000 talents in royal treasures!

142 See *RILR* 84f.

143 Cic. *Att.* vi 1,16.

144 See Cic. *Att.* v 16,2, with Shackleton Bailey's lucid note (p. 218).
Cf. Cic. *fam.* iii 7,3 ; 8,5.

145 It is not clear to what extent the various provisions against
usury applied to these *pactiones*: it may have been in law, as it
certainly was in fact, entirely left up to the governor.

146 Cicero mentions P. Servilius Vatia (*cos.* 78), with surprise.

147 Cic. *Att.* vi 2,5 ; *fam.* ii 13,3.

148 Cic. *Att.* vi 2,5 ; for Verres see 2*Verr.* ii 131f.

149 Cic. *Att.* vi 1,16. For Brutus see ib. 5f.

150 *Att.* vi 1 is written in February 50, only half-way through his
year.

151 Cic. *Att.* v 21,11.

152 Cic. *Att.* vi 1,16: 'habeo in deliciis, obsequor, uerbis laudo, orno,
efficio ne cui molesti sint . . . illa iam habent plena modio [a

reference to heaped measures in paying the tribute grain?—see ch. IV, n. 68]: uerborum honorem, inuitationem crebram.'

153 Cf. the comments of 'some' on Scaptius' refusal of 12 per cent interest: *Att.* v 21,12, *ad fin.*

154 Gabinius seems to have been supported by Syrian embassies (Cic. *Q.fr.* ii 13,2f.), obviously from among the upper class; which is inevitably suspicious, in view of the facts we have about Verres' Sicily and Appius' Cilicia. It may be noted in passing that Appius was consul when they reached Rome: he may have learnt something, if he needed to. (Though he also learnt discretion in applying it.)

155 Cic. *fam.* iii 7,5.

156 The altercation Cic. *Q.fr.,* l.c. (n. 154): Domitius had the impudence to accuse the *equites* of corruption. The scandal Cic. *Att.* iv 15,7; 17,2; *et al.*

157 Brunt, 120: 'their craving for *gratia, auctoritas* and even *honores'.* We should perhaps distinguish: *gratia* and *auctoritas* would be expected, and every *eques Romanus* would to some extent possess them and pride himself on doing so. But even though (as we have seen) entry to the post-Sullan Senate meant fewer sacrifices, the great majority of the equestrian class were not ambitious for public office: they would not dream of wasting their money on election campaigns and the expenses of office, or of giving up their *otium.* Naturally, we hear most about those who *were* ambitious; but the simplest prosopography of late Republican *equites* soon shows that, even so, we know of a massive body who were not; and we must add to it all those of whom we do not even know.

158 Cic. *Att.* vi 1,15 (unfortunately not discussed by Shackleton Bailey). The point of the difference seems to be that Bibulus' wording referred (like the passage of the *Digest* quoted by Shackleton Bailey *ad loc.*) to bad faith or fraud or illegality at the time of the conclusion of the contract. That was an imputation against Roman financiers. Cicero's form (copied from the skilful Scaevola) refers to its being against good faith to *carry out* (or to *recognize*) the agreement—which imputes no motives to those concluding it.

159 See Ürögdi, col. 1201. Crassus' remark most accurately (perhaps) Pliny, *n.h.* xxxiii 134.

160 Cicero, in his speech on behalf of the law of Manilius, stresses the capital investment. As a matter of fact, private citizens who used the banking facilities of the *publicani* (and this must have been much more common than we happen to know) were caught up in their losses. Cicero was one of them (sources ch. IV, nn. 55 and 56).

161 Dio xlii 6,3; cf. App. *b.c.* v 4,19.

162 App. l.c. ; Plut. *Caes.* 48, *init.*

163 Certainly used as propaganda in the speech attributed to Antony (App. l.c.). The facts are not as simple as textbooks copying the information seem to think. Caesar substituted a fixed *tributum* for the variable tithe. It is not asserted that this was calculated at two thirds of the average tithe, i.e. at 6⅔ per cent. What is asserted is that it would mean that the cities would have to *pay* one third less than they had been paying. Caesar may have got that figure from the account books of the *publicani* in the province. But recent accounts would be far from typical, owing to the losses the *publicani* had suffered on account of the Civil War and their consequent attempts to recoup those losses. It is difficult to believe that Caesar conscientiously allowed for this ; easier to think that he remitted a third of the *inflated* (recent) sums, without real loss to the Treasury. It would help to know precisely when this was done. Unfortunately the sources are contradictory and we cannot be sure whether it was before or after the Egyptian campaign, though probably the latter.

164 Cic. *Q.fr.* i 1,33. (Not quite honest in argument ; but the general point must be borne in mind.)

165 See Rostovtzeff, chapters III-VIII ; O. Hirschfeld, *Die kaiserlichen Verwaltungsbeamten*² (1905), 86f. ; de Laet, Part II.

166 Dio xlii 35,5. Perhaps it was in compensation for this (for the Treasury as much as for the *publicani*) that he reintroduced the *portoria* in Italy, abolished as recently as 60 B.C. (Suet. *Jul.* 43 ; cf. de Laet, 60f.).

167 As Cicero had said about the elder Plancius (*Planc.* 32). On the *equites* in Caesar's service see Syme, *Roman Revolution* (1939), ch. V (especially 71f.).

168 See *MRR* ii 188.

169 This story, of the 'equestrian civil service', is told in all the standard works.

170 I should like to thank Professors Sir Ronald Syme and G. V. Sumner for reading the typescript and Mr Christopher Ehrhardt for helping with the proofs. But for Professor Sumner's vigilance, in particular, the number of errors would have been much more numerous than it will in any case turn out to be. None of these scholars should be taken as agreeing with the views expressed. I should also like to thank the Lecture Committee and the University of Otago Press for allowing me to make considerable additions to the lectures (especially to the last of them) and to provide them with notes.

Index of Sources Discussed

This Index collects source passages on which there is some discussion, as distinct from a mere reference. The boundary is inevitably arbitrary.

Index of Names

In this Index, names of places include those of their inhabitants as appropriate: e.g. 'Italy' includes 'Italians'. 'Rome' has not been indexed. Names of persons are given with the highest office (if any) attained, except that anyone who reached the consulship is listed merely with his consulship (his first, where he held several). All Roman names are further provided with their *RE* reference numbers: the articles referred to will be found in the alphabetical sequence, except where a different location is indicated. Non-specific and unimportant references are not analysed. The entry on Cicero includes some important matters on which he is a major source. Some names only mentioned once are omitted, as are listings of general references in phrases like 'Hannibalic War' or 'Macedonian War'. Notes are separately listed where they give additional information.